Pressed Flower Craft

Black base – gold framed circular

Larkspurs have touches of white on the petals which appear at random, as though a paint brush had flicked the petals (this is not so as I never apply colour to any flowers). The contrast of pink and white on a black background makes a bold picture. Lawn daisies and May-weed with their numerous petals give a marked variation to the colourful but stolid outline of candytuft and larkspur. Alyssum, pressed as tiny flowers, makes a pretty white chain. The feathery type of grass was chosen for its effect and being a blend of honey shades, it introduces the yellowish hues of the daisy centres as it links the complete picture. The hair-line stems show up well on the dark background. The addition of dainty grasses to a completed arrangement is time-consuming and requires skilful handling to persuade the tiny wiry pieces to adhere where required. It is worthwhile to experiment by making two similar pictures and adding grasses to one and not the other. I wonder which you will prefer.

Pressed Flower Craft

Joyce Fenton

Midas Books

THE AUTHOR

It was her father, relaxing at weekends on the family farm from his city life as a publisher, who introduced Joyce Fenton to the delights of the countryside at the age of five.

Many years later circumstances brought Joyce to live and teach in Sussex which gave her the opportunity of exploring the South Downs and to renew her love for the countryside.

It was the eldest of her three sons, at that time a geologist in Australia, who presented her with a collage picture made from Australian seeds, thus inspiring her to take up the craft of pressing wild and cultivated flowers, leaves and grasses.

Now resigned from teaching, the author finds the source material for her craft from her garden, where wild flowers flourish, on waste land, window boxes and indoor house plants.

Joyce Fenton.
1981.

Joyce Fenton with the
Mayor of Worthing, 1979.

In the same illustrated Craft Series
Coal Hole Rubbings by Lily Goddard
Photo Montage by Lee Campion
Shell Designs by Christine Haragan

This edition produced 1980 by
Midas Books for
Joyce Fenton,
The Mill, The Street,
Charlwood, Surrey

© Joyce Fenton 1980

ISBN 0 85936 227 2

Designed by Stonecastle Graphics, Tunbridge Wells
Book Production by Chambers Green Ltd, Tunbridge Wells

All rights reserved. No part of this publication
may be reproduced, stored in a retrieval system,
or transmitted, in any form or by any means,
electronic, mechanical, photocopying, recording or
otherwise, without the prior permission of Midas Books.

Printed in England by Pindar Print Limited,
Scarborough, North Yorkshire

Front cover:

The single pansy is
surrounded by a flow of
wild clematis leaves (old
man's beard) connected by
wild radish and corn
chamomile with sprays of
quaking grass, mounted on
pale blue satin under non-
reflective glass.

Back cover:

Rectangle: A single
celandine, small daisies and
wild cabbage combined with
wild clematis leaves and
grasses blend spring and
early summer into a gay
little picture.

Oval: The tiny leaves of elm
have been preserved in this
gentle spray of perennial
cornflower, lobelia flowers
and grey hair-grass.

Contents

1 Picking 9

2 Pressing 17

3 Design 29

4 Miniatures 41

5 Canadian and Australian pictures 45

6 Fixing pressed materials 50

7 Framing 59

8 Grow your own wild flowers 65

9 Picking and pressing through the seasons 67

Chapter 1

PICKING

You will need:
Polythene bags of various sizes
Cardboard box to fit base of large bag
Small sharp scissors
Press or telephone directory (see Chapter 2)

Picking away from home

It is essential to remember that the world of floral beauty is for all to enjoy; therefore, picking wild flowers must be done with great care to avoid damage to the plant and root. If too many flowers are picked from one plant, this will not only deny other people the pleasure of seeing them growing but, in some cases, may even check propagation or further increase of the species. Avoid picking buds – they will later become flowers – and above all do not pick rarities, orchids and, in certain areas, diminishing primroses. (*See list, Chapter 9*).

I recall, a day in June, admiring a stretch of rough ground full of wild treasures on a golf-course, and orchids around the edges. I picked a few ox-eye daises, vetch clovers and campions and returned next day to find the area had been mown flat, the orchids left dying where the machine had flattened them! On another occasion, early one morning in July, I had a remarkable find; a piece of ground had been slightly hollowed out, turf removed for use elsewhere and a profusion of wild flowers had taken over – a perfect garden in which melilot, toad-flax, knapweed, St John's wort, white campion, fumitory, convolvulus,

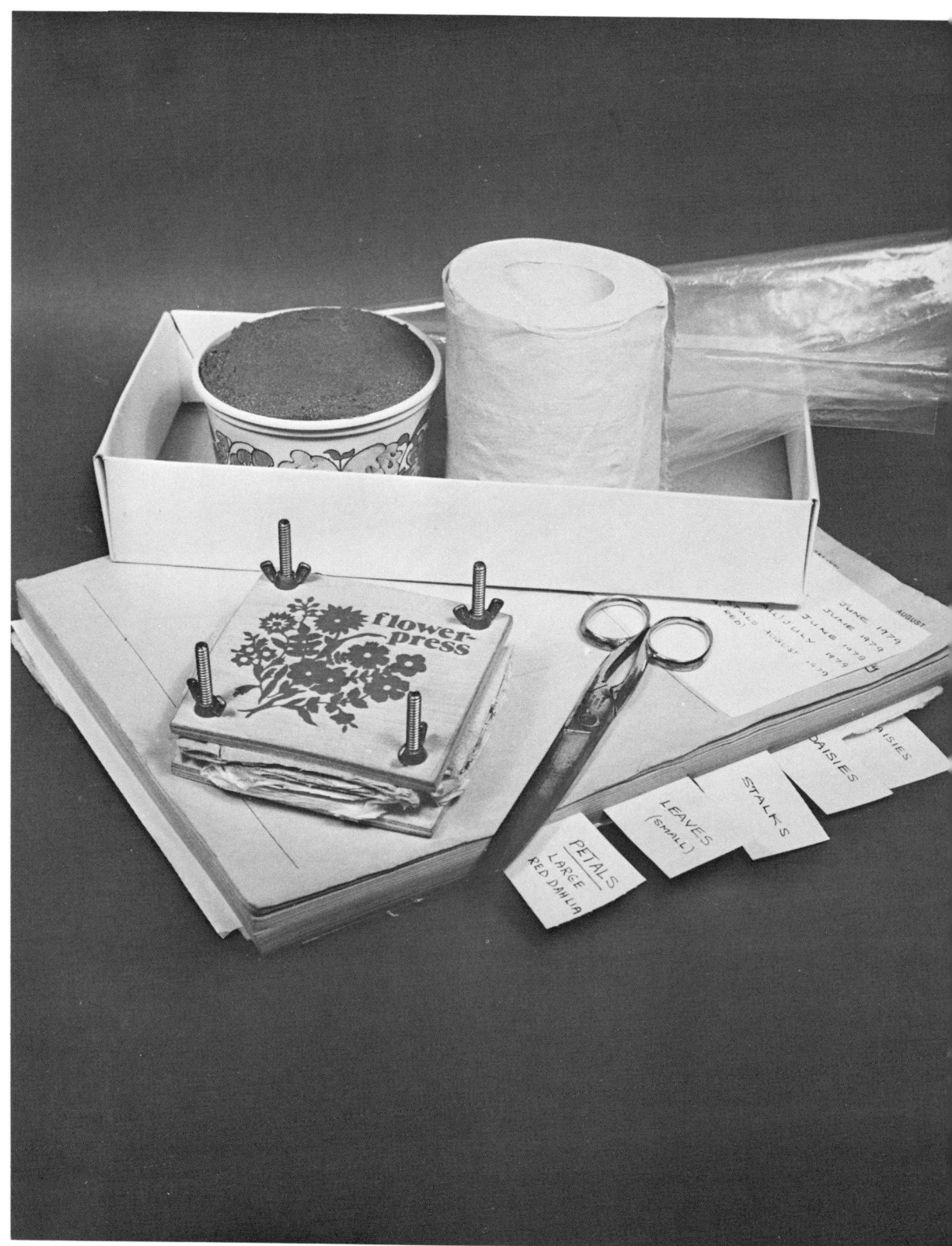

ragwort, mayweed, chamomile, mignonette, and yellow bedstraw grew happily together. In the morning sunshine the delicate blending of colour and perfume left me with a memory to be cherished and a scene to return to later in the day, when early morning dew had been absorbed and dried by the sun and air, and the flowers would be ready for picking and pressing.

The time to pick is when the flowers are free of moisture on their petals. Moisture causes mould or loss of colour. The recommended time on a sunny summer's day is coffee-time, between 10 and 11 am, when the sun has sufficiently dried the flowers but not overheated and wilted them. If the morning is showery or misty, allow a time of sunshine before picking in late afternoon. When picking wild flowers use a bag containing a box – the box keeps the sides of the bag apart and avoids flowers pressing into condensation which will possibly form on the inside of the bag. Keep the bag closed by holding the top together, but not fastened to exclude air circulation. I learnt from bitter experience that if I held the bag at only one spot a breeze could remove the contents of a few flowers and by the end of my walk I was holding an empty bag!

Never pick more than you know you are able to press in the time available when you return home, or to your car.

Set all you have picked on a towel or cloth for a short while to dry off any condensation from the bag, or put them in a container of water – making sure stalks or flowers required for pressing are not in the water. Do not leave flowers too long; once they begin to wilt they are useless.

If you have gone by car to a point near your picking area, you can either pick one type of flower, grass or leaf at a time, return to the car and press, or have a container (*eg* a margarine tub) filled with wet oasis which will help to keep them fresh for a longer period until you get home – but don't push your luck! All flowers of the umbellifer family – easily recognised by their umbrella shape – cow parsley, hedge parsley, fennel, hogweed; fairy flax and stitchwort, wilt very quickly.

Garden and window-box picking

This offers you the opportunity to judge more easily the condition of the flowers. Watching their growth, you will come to know how long the flowers have been blooming. The centre of a lawn daisy, for instance, will show you by its cushioned centre of stamens if it has been out some days. As it opens the centre of any daisy type of flower gradually develops its stamens to open and attract the bees. It will soon become a habit to distinguish between freshly opened flowers and those beginning to fade, deteriorating with darkening centres or fading petals. Regarding your plants with pressing in mind will give added interest and bring daily discoveries which I have found to be exciting.

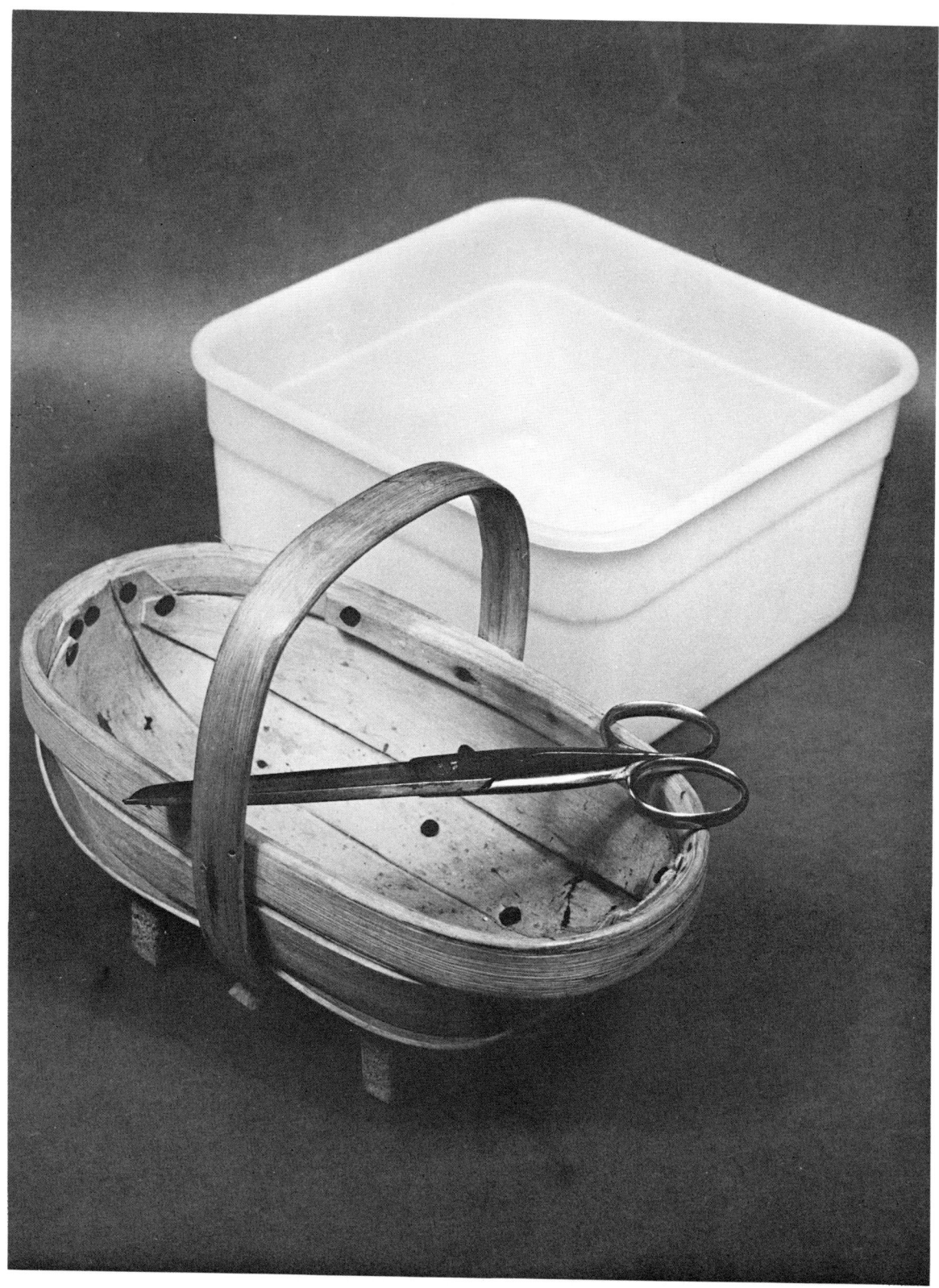

Experiment with all house plants – African violet, geranium, fuchsia, pelargonium, begonia (offer interest if they are small), variegated leaves, cyclamen, azalea, primula, bougainvillea (excellent), ferns, achimenes.

Pick only fresh flowers: a few examples

Buttercup. If the centre of a buttercup is hard to the touch it is beginning to go to seed; leave it, look for buttercups with soft buttery stamens, these are excellent and you can be sure of good pressing results. Pick the leaves, too.

Clover. The lower flowers should be removed if brown and only the top cluster of white or red clover should be used.

Daisy. The yellow centres of all daisy types should be firm. Look closely and you will notice that it is possible to tell the difference between one just opened and one which has been open a few days by the development of the stamens.

Bladder Campion. Pressing the calyx which is the container which holds the seeds, you will find the difference between a fresh and old flower. If you feel a hard lump inside when gently pressing between finger and thumb, leave it; the lump inside will prevent the case from pressing and will result in a crinkled mass; whereas if the seeds are not developing, the bladder, which is beautifully marked, will press well.

Forget-me-not. If the flower drops off when lightly touched, leaving a tiny stem, the seed is already developing and the flower has been in bloom too long. Pick only each tiny flower nearest to unopened buds.

In many flowers, too numerous to list, the little stamens change colour by darkening as they age.

Leaves. Do not overlook the infinite variety of leaves which will enhance your pictures. Cow parsley leaves appear bright green and feathery in profusion and are of the first for picking on a dry day. The leaves of trees must be picked young before they become too fleshy, unless you are fortunate enough to find a later growth round the base of a tree during later summer. Pick a variety of all trees and shrubs to experiment with colour change and variation of vein formation under press. You will require a wide range of shape and colour. Yarrow leaf, old man's beard with curvy stem, all types of grey leaves, circular leaf of Crane's bill, or the spiky 'old man' if separated (*see illustration: Chapter 2*). Look for unusual shapes, interest in veining (some show more clearly than others). Sometimes stinging nettles will have quite yellow leaves with dark veins, cow parsley leaves may become purple at the base of the plant, wild rose leaves a delicate yellow. Blackberry leaves offer a wide selection of colour throughout the year from brilliant yellow-honey colour to gentle browns. Young beech leaves are fringed with a silver hair-like edge which shows up when mounted on a dark background.

Flowers and seeds of trees. Catkins and ash seeds: pick young. Pick as many leaves as you do flowers, of the widest possible variety, and you will be amazed at the discoveries you make. In your garden you will be growing plants to pick for their leaf interest.

Garden flowers. All flowers are suitable for picking, but the technique of pressing is important to give the desired result of a perfect form to use in a picture (*See pressing: Chapter 2*).

Grasses. Never forget these. Late May and June is the time to pick them. Scissors are not necessary – they can be pulled. There is a large variety of shape and colour to be found wherever they are allowed to grow in the garden, hedgerow, field or waste-land. Pick when fully out, rather than massed thickly up the stem, shake out any tiny seed. Quaking grass is pretty but may be too bulky under glass.

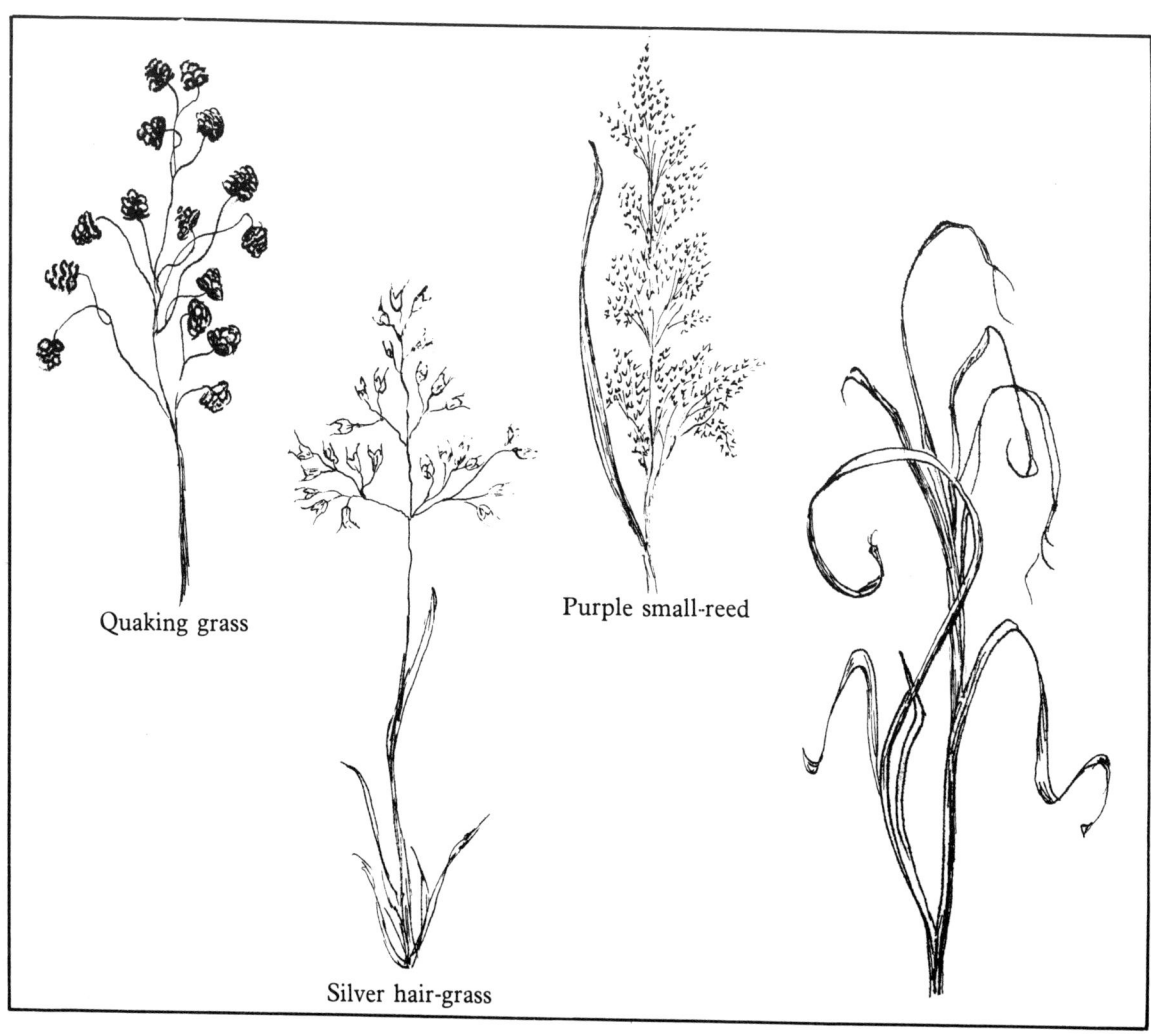

Quaking grass

Purple small-reed

Silver hair-grass

Picking through the seasons

Spring

In the garden. The earliest blooms are attractive to capture for pressing – snowdrop, daffodil, crocus, violet, primrose, grape hyacinth, hyacinth, and all that heralds spring. At this time of year it is often very showery and damp. So allow time in the house for flowers to dry as much as possible, and be prepared for disappointments unless a dry spell has preceded your picking.

Bluebells, or dark violets can be successfully pressed when picked during a dry spell.

Weather conditions and conservation prevent the gathering of wild flowers for pressing at this time of year. Tempting as it may be to pick primroses and cowslips, their attractive yellow flowers should be admired only and left alone. Wood anemones, violets and bluebells are invariably disappointing when pressed.

Summer – April to September

Around St George's Day be ready to pick dandelions. So many common flowers of the field and hedgerow are excellent for pressing in early summer: buttercup, daisies of all kinds, elder flower, vetches, clovers, cow-parsley, lady's smock, Queen Anne's lace, trefoils, wild cabbage, milkwort, thistles, willowherb. Pick flowers of stinging nettles; they won't hurt your fingers, but may sting your legs!

Old man's beard, or traveller's joy, needs special mention. The leaves mentioned under the leaf heading are ready to pick as soon as the first shoots appear in May on the hedgerows. As they are used to

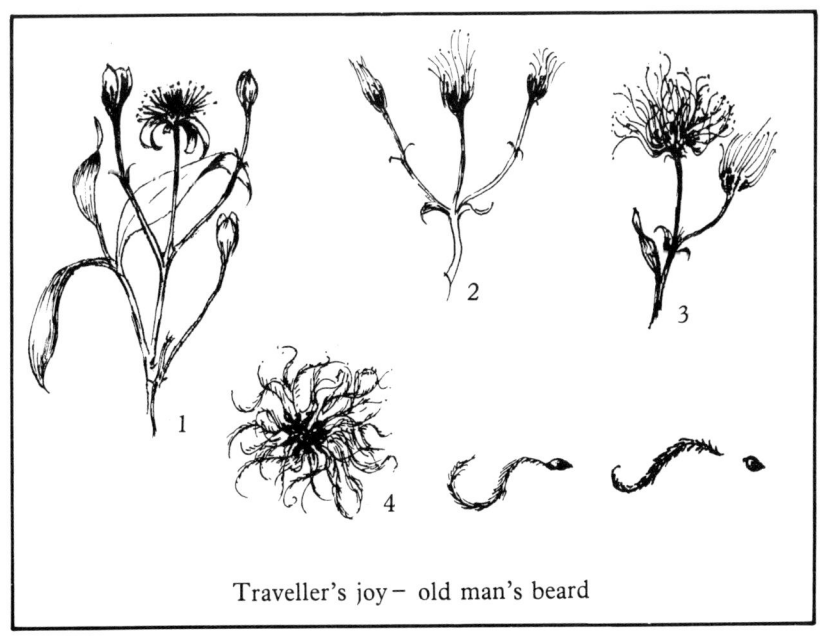

Traveller's joy – old man's beard

support the plant the stalks take on excellent curves with a leaf at the end and two leaves an inch or two further down. Cut below these which will give three leaves on a dark stem with a pleasing curve. At the end of July, the first flowers appear, spikey and creamy in colour, followed in late August by the first signs of what in winter months will grace the hedges as grey 'fluff'. At every stage of this attractive plant it can be used in a variety of ways: the early green silky seed conveyors and the later grey may be pressed, as well as the first blooms.

Special note on all flowers, leaves and grasses: after picking, all can be 'broken down' therefore it is possible to experiment with anything that appeals for colour, shape or texture.

Autumn

By September the wild flowers are over, but some may be enjoying a second budding. If you have discovered the soft spray of green flowers of the stinging nettles, you will notice other plants usually growing on rough ground with similar spikes of greyish green available to pick in September: pick off the main stalk, they will form interesting shapes under press.

Pick thistles with scissors when they are almost dead. They can be painful to the fingers. Pull them apart; the 'down' can be pressed.

As the days become shorter, picking time for late garden flowers is nearer tea-time than coffee-time. Late on a sunny day, as morning dews are often very heavy, small flowers like lobelia, tagettees, alyssum, will still press well. Pick dahlias, fuchsias, marigolds; keep them indoors in water for twelve hours before pressing, allowing them to lose surplus moisture.

Autumn leaves are always attractive, retaining their colour well. Pick all shapes, sizes and colours; if they are damp, even picked up off the ground, provided they are not shrivelling. The pressed result should not be disappointing. Enjoy the galaxy of autumn hues!

Chapter 2

PRESSING

You will need:
Small pointed scissors
Stanley knife
Absorbent toilet paper (blotting paper, or typing paper may be used but are expensive)
Newspapers
Press (optional)
Old telephone directory

The object of pressing is to retain the shape and colour, excluding air and drying out the plant materials for use in floral designs. The colour of a pressed flower, leaf, fern or moss will not be exactly the same as when the plant material is growing, due to the absence of moisture. As a general guide this list may be helpful but as I have experienced many surprises you will doubtless find the same fascination of never quite knowing the result of your pressing. See page 70 for detailed guide.

White wild flowers
   Retaining whiteness: daisy, cow-parsley, fairyflax, mayweed, stitchwort, small shrub flowers.
   Turning cream or honey-coloured: hogweed, clover, dead-nettle, bind weed.

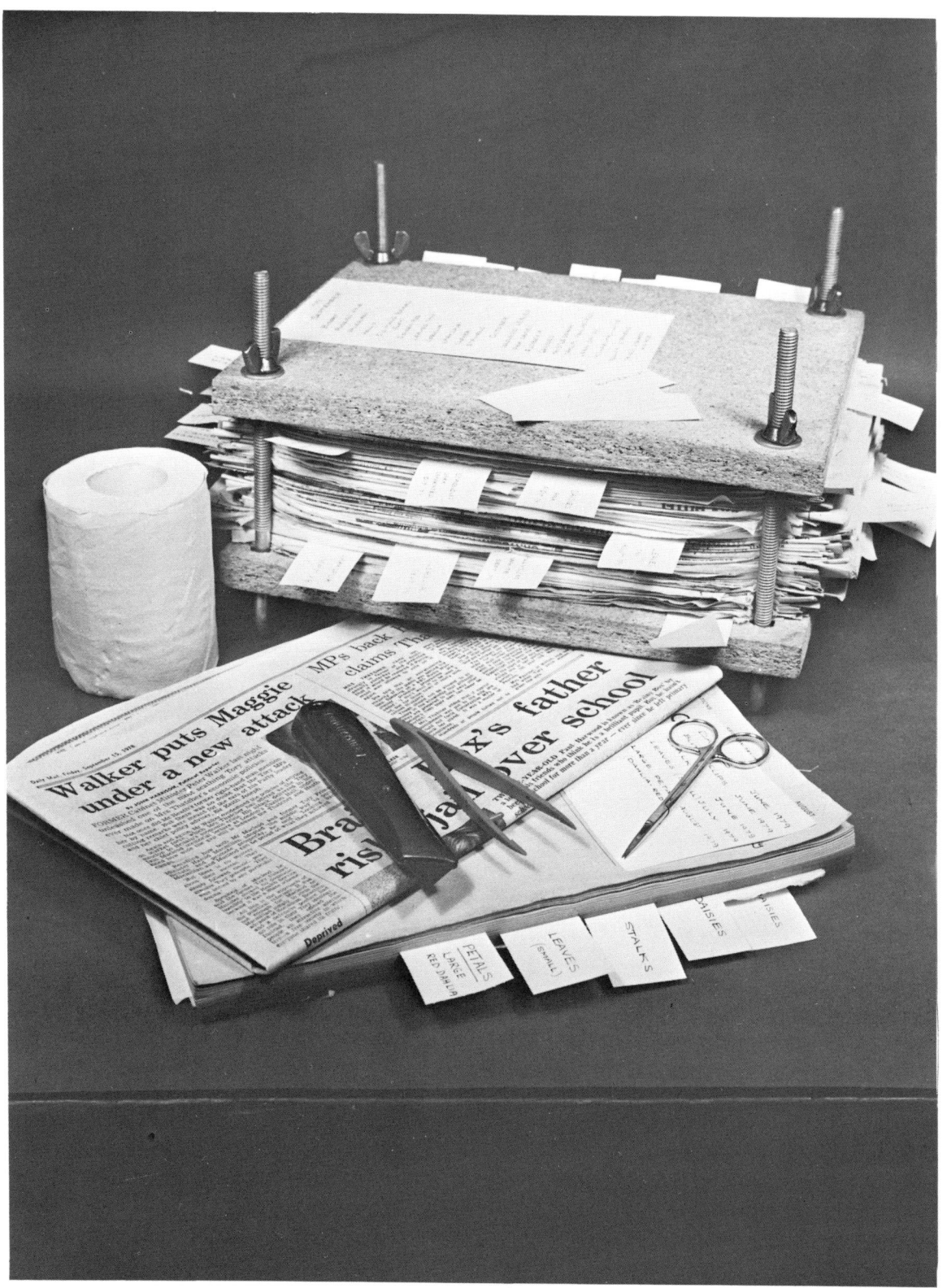

White garden flowers

Retaining whiteness: daisy, alyssum, candytuft, larkspur, many small shrub flowers.

Turning cream or honey-coloured: rose, dahlia, syringa, large shrub flowers.

Yellow wild flowers

Retaining yellow: dandelion family, buttercup, St John's Wort, cinquefoil, corydalis, mustard family, cabbage family, melilot, broom, yellow pea, horseshoe vetch, hog's fennel, ragwort.

Turning cream or honey-coloured: gorse; bird's foot trefoil often turns green.

As previously mentioned, the flowers should be pressed as soon as possible after picking, provided they are not wet, and if you take a press with you on a walk, remember the slightest breeze is a major hazard as you press on the spot – so unless the day is quite 'still' use the protection of a car or take your treasures home to press. Even at home beware of an open door or window!

Pressing and excluding air can be achieved by very economical means, *ie* newspaper and toilet paper, old telephone directory (two sheets of loo-paper exactly fits page size), or home-made press. If, however, you already have a shop press it must be stressed that newspaper should be added – about four pieces cut to the shape of blotting paper and corrugated card already provided. Insert the four layers of newspaper between a piece of card and blotting paper to avoid 'ripples' on the petals or leaves.

Newspaper method

A cupboard top or shelf, the size of your daily paper, which may be left undisturbed for some months, makes storage easy. Have a sheet of hardboard cut to the size of the newspapers you are likely to use, and use either a couple of bricks or some heavy household article as a weight.

Open the dry newspaper – I usually iron mine to get it flat – at the centre page, cover one side with three strips of toilet paper the same length, place these just to lap over slightly. Set flowers or leaves in place (not touching), cover with three more strips of loo-paper, close newspaper, place hardboard and then brick or weight on top. So simple; just continue to add newspapers in the same way, building up.

Label newspaper or add a slip of paper to protrude with name for easy selection later.

Telephone directory

By 'pressing' from the back of the old book and leaving about 12 pages between each pressing, it is possible to fill it with a quantity of materials.

Place telephone directory on a table, open it at the back, support the rest against something to keep it flat. Loo-paper is then placed in two strips of two pieces on the telephone directory page ('Wilson' approximately!) slightly over-lapping. Add the flowers, repeat loo-paper and close another 12 pages. Repeat as necessary. Close directory carefully and store with heavy weight on top. Add as required until full.

Either stick a label on the outside and add the names of pressed flowers from bottom to top of label, or place indicating strips of paper down the side of the telephone directory just protruding 2.5cm (1in) with names of contents, staggered for easy reference.

Home made press

Use chipboard as plywood may bend under pressure. Get two pieces of 1.5cm (¾in) chipboard cut at your local DIY shop to approximately 25cm by 50cm (10in by 20in) with four 1.2cm (½in) diameter holes drilled 2.5cm (1in) in from each side. This can now be secured with 4 wing nuts, 4 wire stretchers (used for chain link fences) 20cm (7.8in) long, and 4 washers.

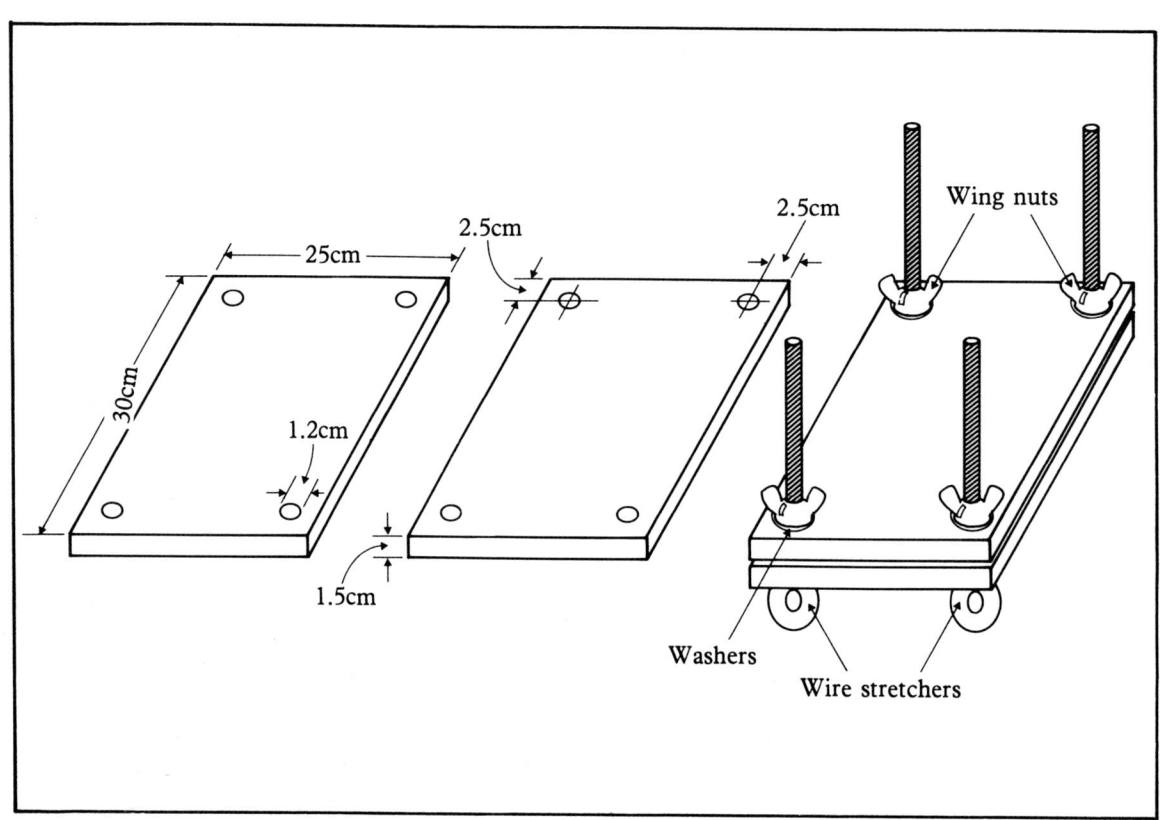

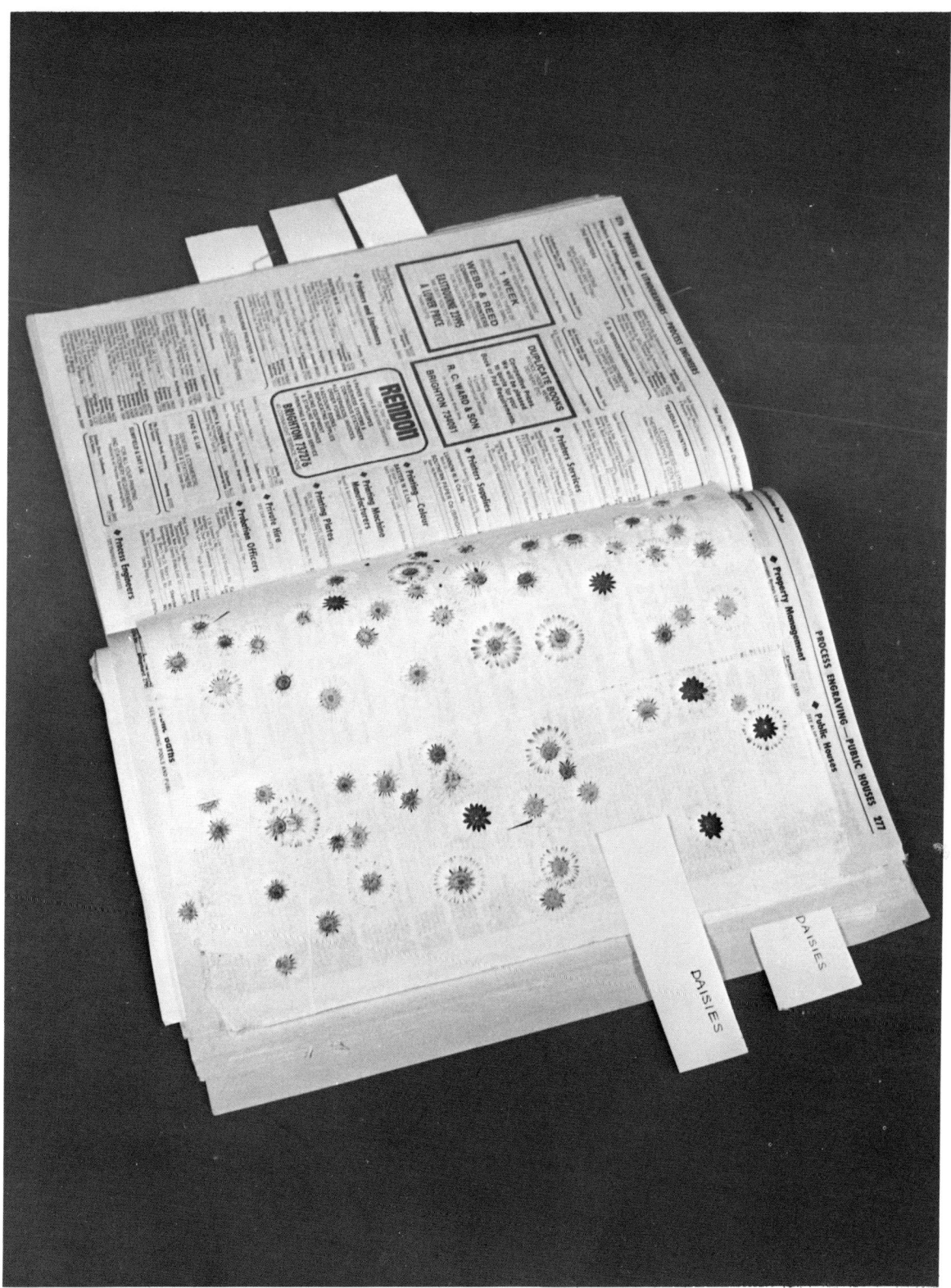

Your press is then built up with layers of dry folded newspapers; a small newspaper folds exactly into four if you fold each double sheet in half. The easiest way to do this is to begin at the centre of the newspaper, fold over to make two sheets, then fold in half, and iron over to remove any dampness and make the folded paper smooth. Continue in this way through the newspaper. With a neat pile of folded paper and a toilet roll you are now ready to get pressing. Make sure the paper fits between the screws without rucking; trim to fit if necessary.

Place folded newspaper on base and cover this with two strips of

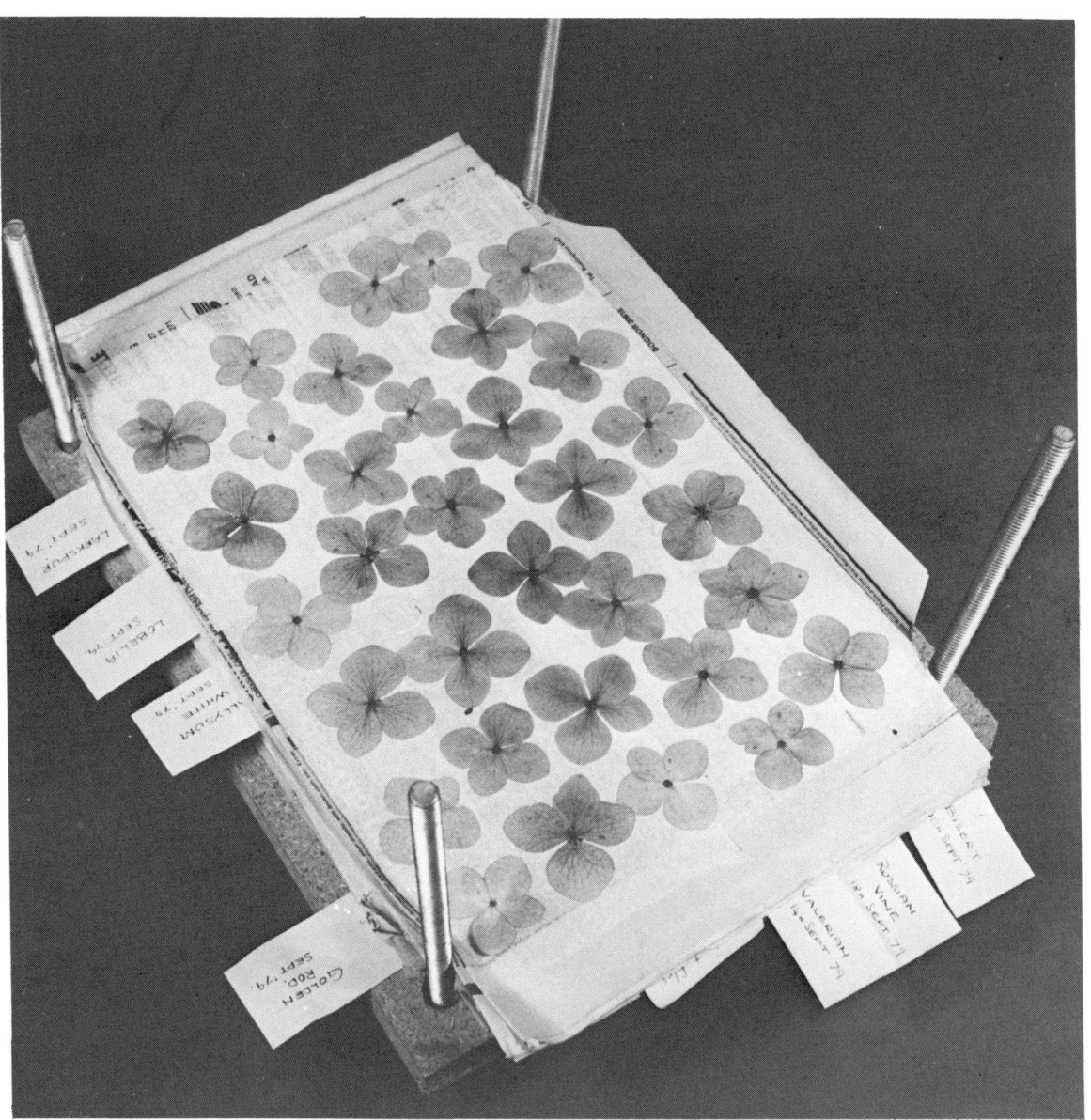

absorbent loo-paper, add flowers, cover with two more strips of loo-paper, then newspaper. If the flowers or leaves seem bulky, add more newspaper before repeating the process.

Flowers, leaves and ferns should be left undisturbed for at least six weeks; the longer they are under press the longer they will retain colour when used decoratively. Pressure must be consistent – someone told me their flowers were under the carpet and I asked if they stood permanently on the spot! Depending on passing traffic is not the way to satisfactory results.

Some flowers contain more moisture than others. If you open your

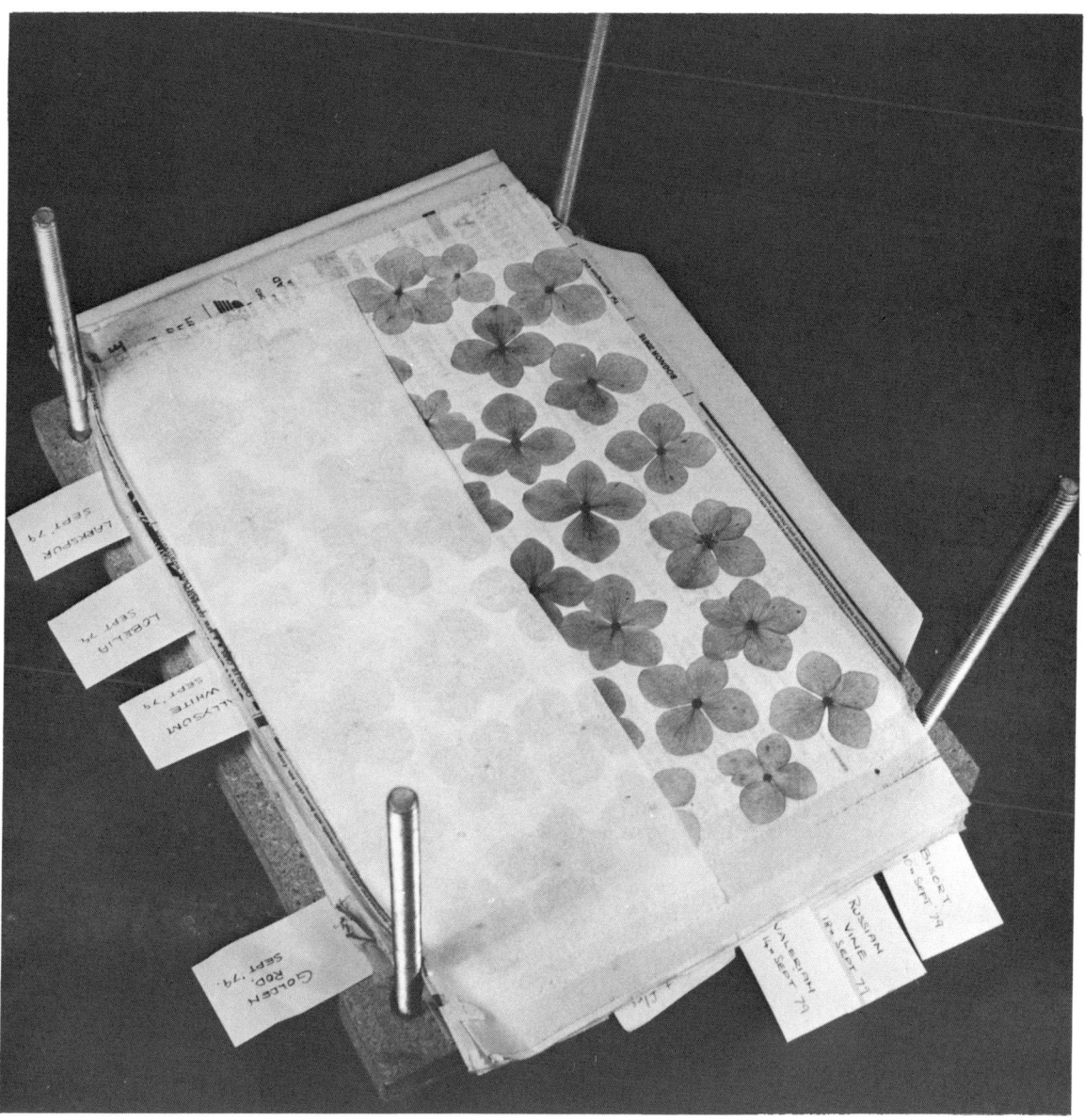

Pansy

press after two days and find the newspaper is damp, remove it and replace with fresh paper, but do not disturb the flowers between the loo-paper. Keep presses in a dry, well ventilated room, or even the airing cupboard, but do not put it in the garden shed or loft. In the summer I move presses from room to room, chasing warmth from the sun to hasten the process.

Labelling

Labelling is important. It saves time when you require a particular flower. Give the name, colour and date as these identify the flowers and tell you how long they have been pressed. This information can be written on small slips of paper about 5cm (2in) long, 4 cm (1½in) wide. Put the label inside the folded newspaper above the flower. If you place the next label between next layer above, 12mm (½in) further to the right and so on up the press, you will find it easier when looking for specific flowers when you are picture-making. Remember you have four sides to your press — each side can hold the tags.

An alternative is to fix a strip of paper the length of your press and 10cm (4in) or 13cm (5in) wide to the top piece of chipboard. Enter the name, colour, date, starting at the bottom of strip and working upwards; this will help you when selecting pressed materials, as those on the top of the list will be on the top layer of the press, and so on.

Pressing Flowers

Firstly remove thick stalks. This means that most stalks are in this category and should be pressed separately. With sharp, pointed scissors, snip stalk very close to the flower.

Do not mix different types of flowers on one page, otherwise you get thicker ones pressed and those with finer petals will go shrivelly — a horrible sight when you want them for a picture!

Avoid thick centres. Sometimes these may be dealt with by removing the bulk with a Stanley knife. As an example, the Japanese anemone has a bulbous green centre which is easily cut flat by slicing through very carefully to avoid damaging the little stamens.

Fuchsia can be pressed by slicing through, which will give two flowers, OR TAKE IT APART (*see illustration*).

Love-in-a-mist develop seeds on the top of the flower and these can be felt gently with your finger. This, too, can be carefully removed.

Place flowers face down on loo-paper, making sure petals are flat, and press down gently on the centre with your finger to give a start to pressing.

Allow sufficient space between flowers to avoid overlapping when pressure is applied. Petals may be removed and pressed separately as for dahlias, large daisies, zinnias, carnations and marigolds. The stamens of these flowers may be pressed separately on another sheet. The sepals of dahlias press well (*see illustration*). To remove petals, roll

Japanese anemone

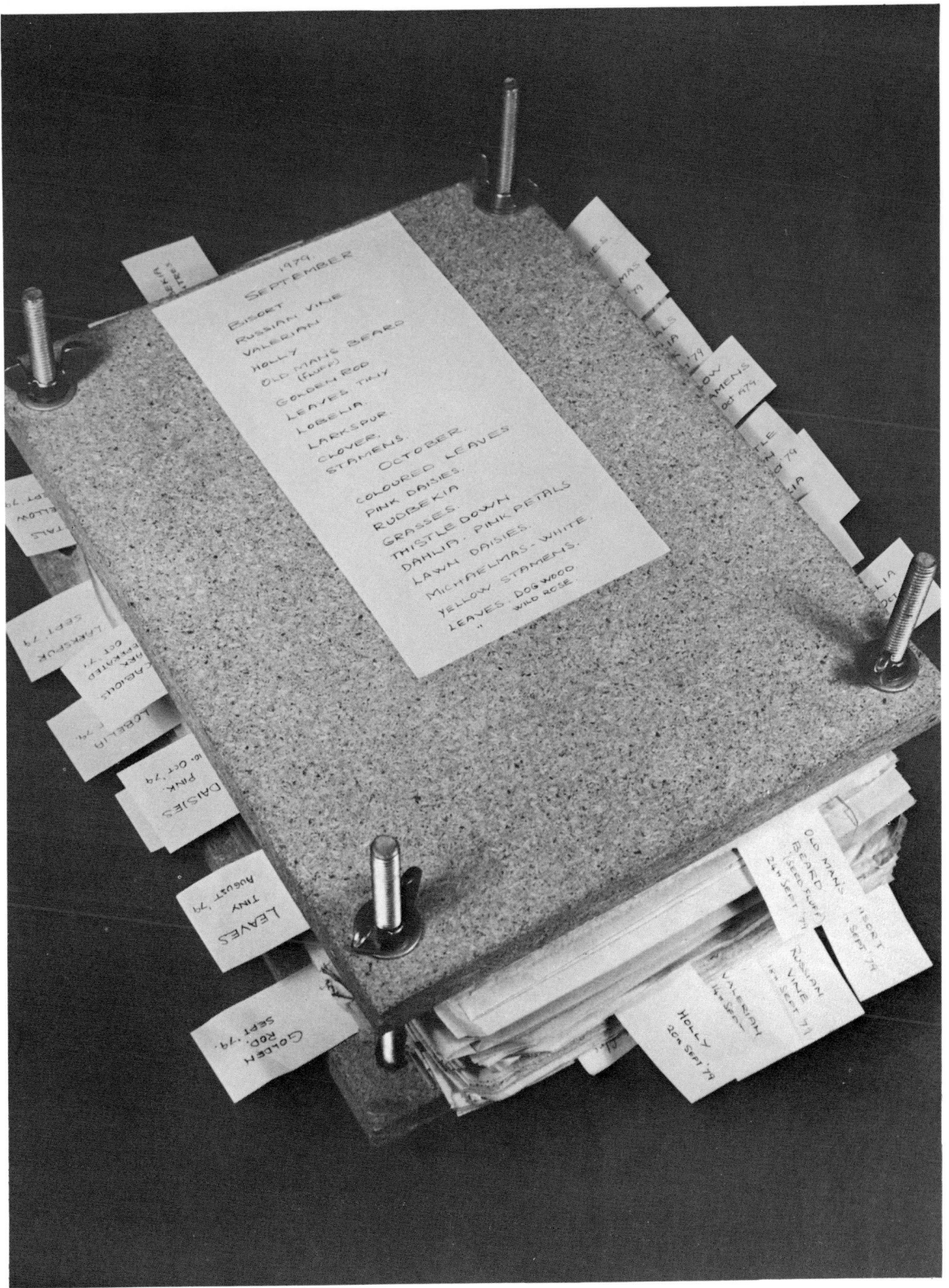

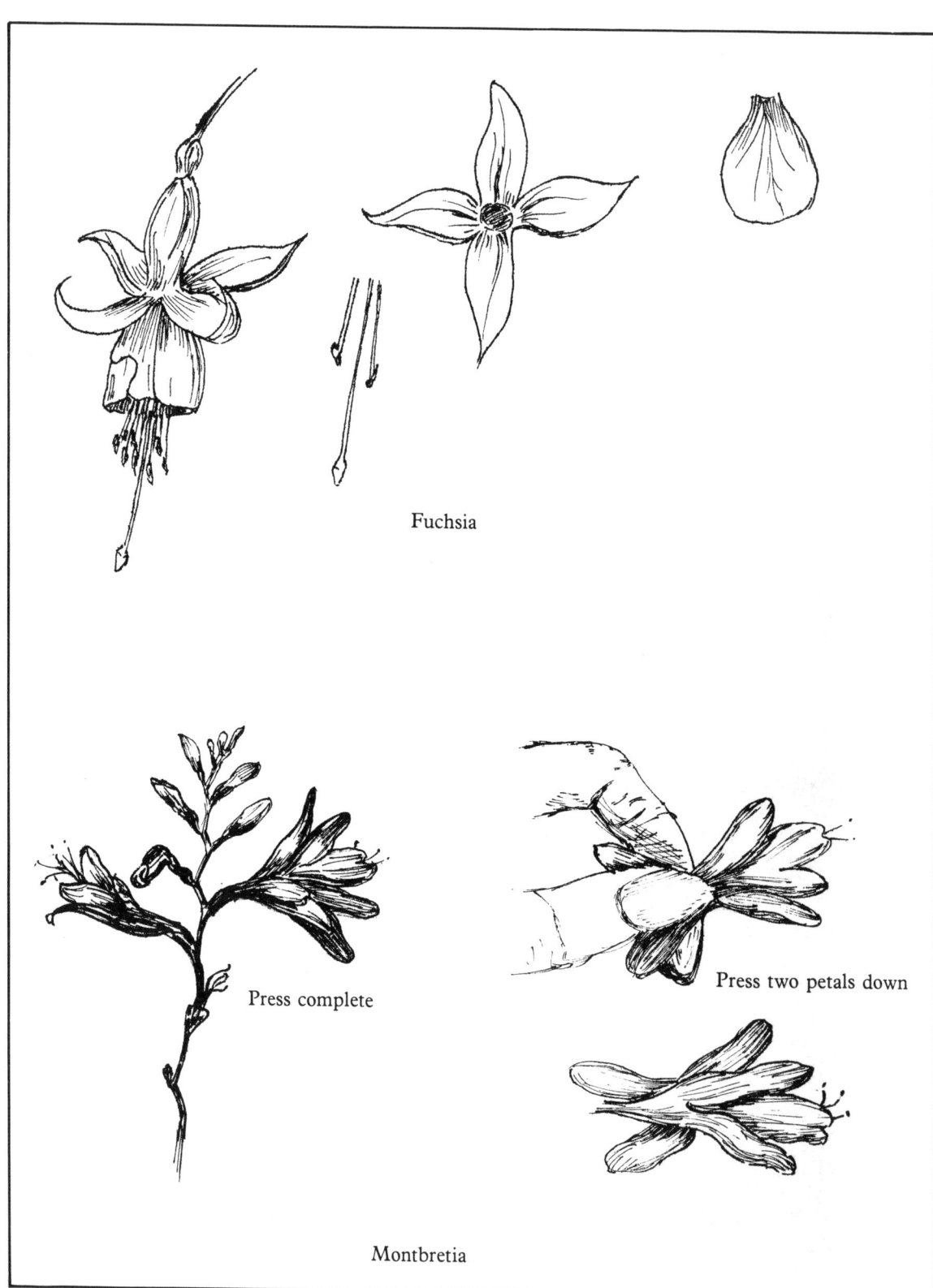

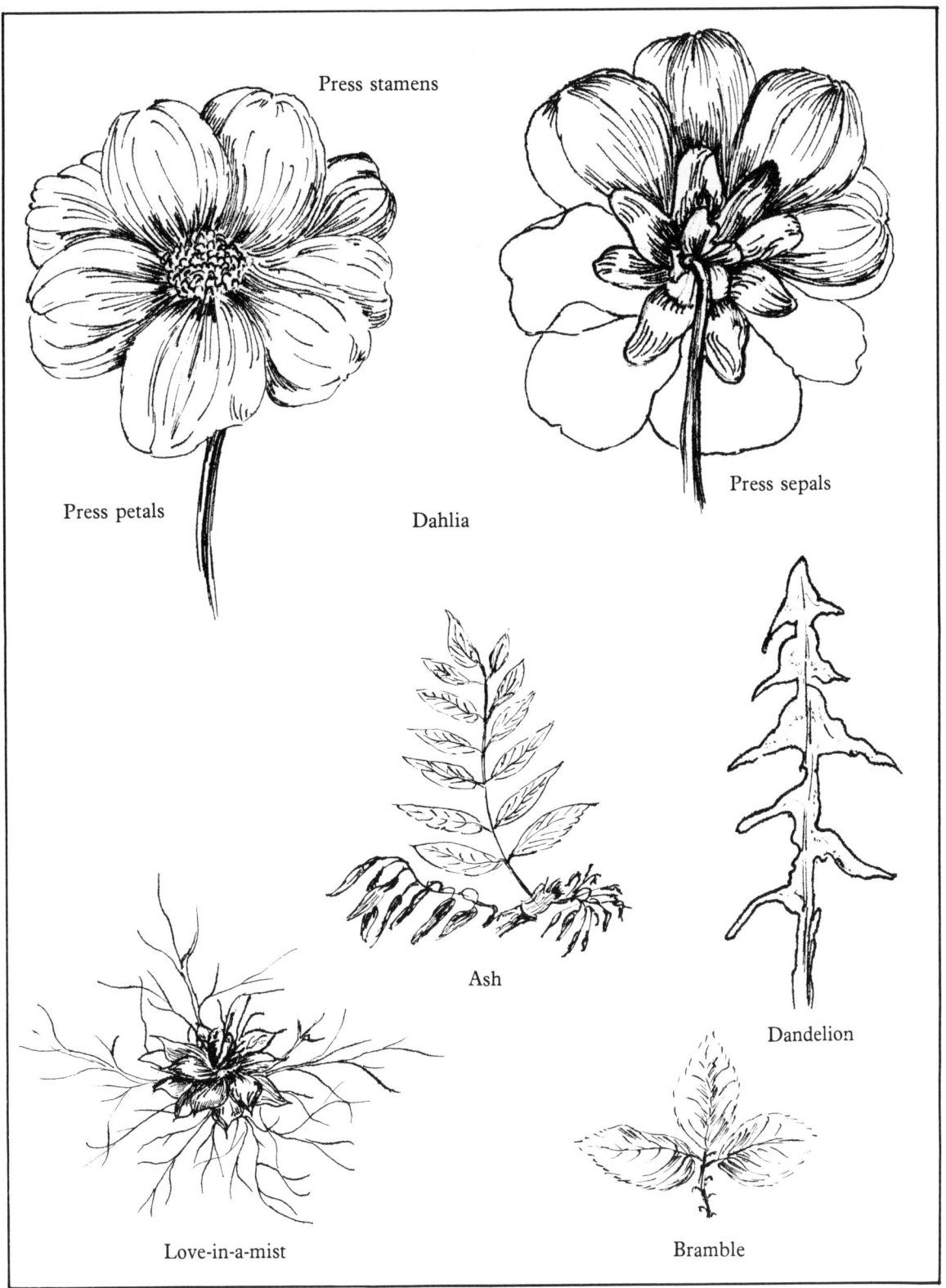

Old man

Traveller's joy – old man's beard

the calyx between finger and thumb; this will loosen the whole flower.

Montbretia and other freesia type of flowers should be eased from the calyx and pressed by folding back two petals. Hold these between finger and thumb as the flower is placed face down on the loo-paper and covered quickly before the flower can resume its normal shape.

Leaves may be pressed throughout the year. Tree leaves should be young or turning colour. The leaves of plants may be mature.

The rule of similar thickness to a page applies. Remove thick stems close to leaf. Allow space between the leaves. By experimenting you will find groups of leaves on a stem may be satisfactorily pressed as in bramble, ash, or old man's beard. Young ash seeds turn black when pressed and are very useful. If leaves are turning red they may be pressed even if damp; if loo-paper is not used, they press well between newspaper.

Creepers. The glorious reds of virginia creeper are so attractive as you set them out in your press on their stems, provided the stem is not thick. To be certain the leaves are well pressed, remove from the stems and press separately; it is so disappointing if the leaves are not perfectly smooth when you remove them for use in a picture.

Ferns. Select types to press together as they vary greatly in thickness. Remove any thick stems and press fern separately but, in many cases, they are easily pressed complete. Bracken, unless pressed green, is too dry and brittle.

Grasses. These may be pressed in newspaper only. Spread each head of grass and curve the stalk if possible, after trimming it to fit the press or telephone directory. Sort out your grass collection before pressing and place grass of same thickness on a page; overlapping will not spoil the results.

Chapter 3

DESIGN

After many hours spent picking and pressing and six weeks of waiting, anxiously wondering what you will see when the press is opened, the time has arrived for designing a picture, calendar, book mark or greetings card.

It is well to recall that when picking the flowers, leaves and grasses, you noticed that stalks or stems very rarely grew exactly horizontal or vertical to the ground or plant.

Although plants may grow straight stems, it is rare to see these growing at right angles to the soil, unless tied to a supporting stick, and the flowers on the stem take a slightly different direction. It is interesting to look at growing plants with this point in mind.

And so, when making a picture – large, small, oval or square – it is so important to get the effect of being together to form a pleasing composition which looks natural. This is a craft in which the designer has the unique opportunity of expressing individual style and original ideas which are endless, inspired by the beauty of materials provided by nature. But unless the beginner has a few basic guide lines the first attempts may be disappointing. The aim of this chapter is to help and encourage you to satisfaction in your first steps. From experience over the years, I have realised that a style of design which is pleasing to me is not necessarily likely to please others and so, by experimenting and expanding, I have discovered a variety of ways of creating my pictures which I hope will appeal to others. These include the flowers blooming from a growing point, sprays, clusters, and symmetrical designs. (*See coloured plates, Nos. 1-12*).

In my first enthusiasm, the pictures I made contained a profusion of colour, shape and texture – I simply did not know where to stop!

On one occasion I proudly sought my son's approval of what, to me,

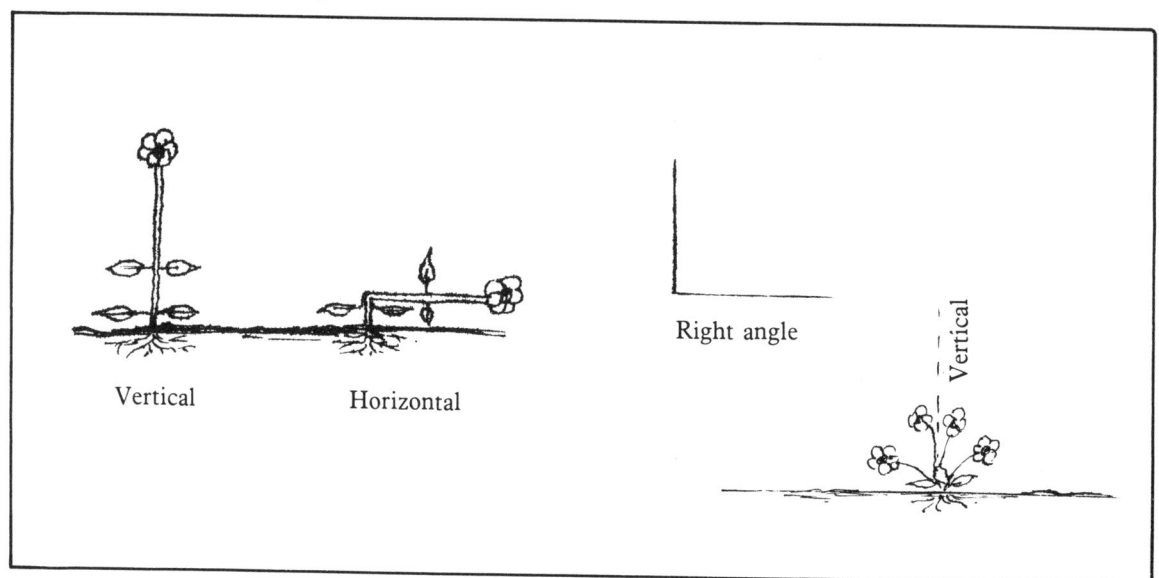

Vertical   Horizontal   Right angle   Vertical

looked like a nice picture. His comment after consideration was not only honest – it taught me a lesson – 'It's too mixed up and cluttered'.

When the flowers of your choice have been removed from the press, place them on the background you intend to use. Is the colour suitable? A large flower may take too much space, not allowing for leaves to be added. Tiny flowers may not give enough colour in a large arrangement. Select a variety of colours or tones; start by limiting it to three colours, and that includes white flowers. The pronounced outline of buttercups contrasts well with the lawn daisies' little petals; forget-me-nots introduce a smaller linking flower. (*See page 35* and the addition of leaves and grasses).

Useful guidelines for beginners

(i) Take a piece of notepaper – unlined – to practise on. Use tweezers if you prefer this method of handling flowers to using fingers.

(ii) Work with odd numbers – 3 buttercups, 3 daisies and an odd number of leaves – 3, 5 or 7. To begin with, use only flowers of varying sizes, without stems.

(iii) Place your flowers to form a series of triangles. It is not always advisable to place your leaves first. Practise moving them around to form a variety of triangles. If you use a small paint brush for this it saves handling the flowers too much. Horizontal and vertical lines must be avoided.

(iv) In most arrangements the outline at the bottom of the picture should be greater than the rest of the planned group. If you experiment later with a trailing spray this may well flow from a cluster of flowers at the top of a picture, but as I am writing for the beginner this will not be dealt with here.

The outline sketches are diagramatical and you may like to trace the triangles with your finger and see how many you can make in each of my sketches.

By placing the largest leaves and flowers at the bottom and graduating them upwards, a lighter effect towards the top of the arrangement will give the best results. Designs which radiate from a focal feature are graceful and restful. The feature may be a group of leaves, flowers and leaves, or one large flower and leaves.

(v) A margin is very important, so keep in mind the width of this – it is only imaginary – do not draw one. Never allow any pressed material to extend to the edge of the card or other material on which you are working. As a beginner it may be helpful to make a guide by cutting strips of paper to place on your background, particularly in the case of a picture, when the arrangement must *never* touch the frame line. The distance from the sides should be the same, but the bottom and/or top may be wider. This rule applies to greetings cards, book marks, finger plates, etc. As experience is gained this will not be necessary, as you will find you can judge the distances without the use of paper strips to guide you.

(vi) Avoid placing anything exactly central. It will create a cut-in-half effect which is easily avoided by a fractional movement to left or right of imaginary centre line. In the illustrations notice the dotted centre line. *No. 1:* the centre is fractionally avoided; in *No. 2* I am sure you will spot many deliberate mistakes.

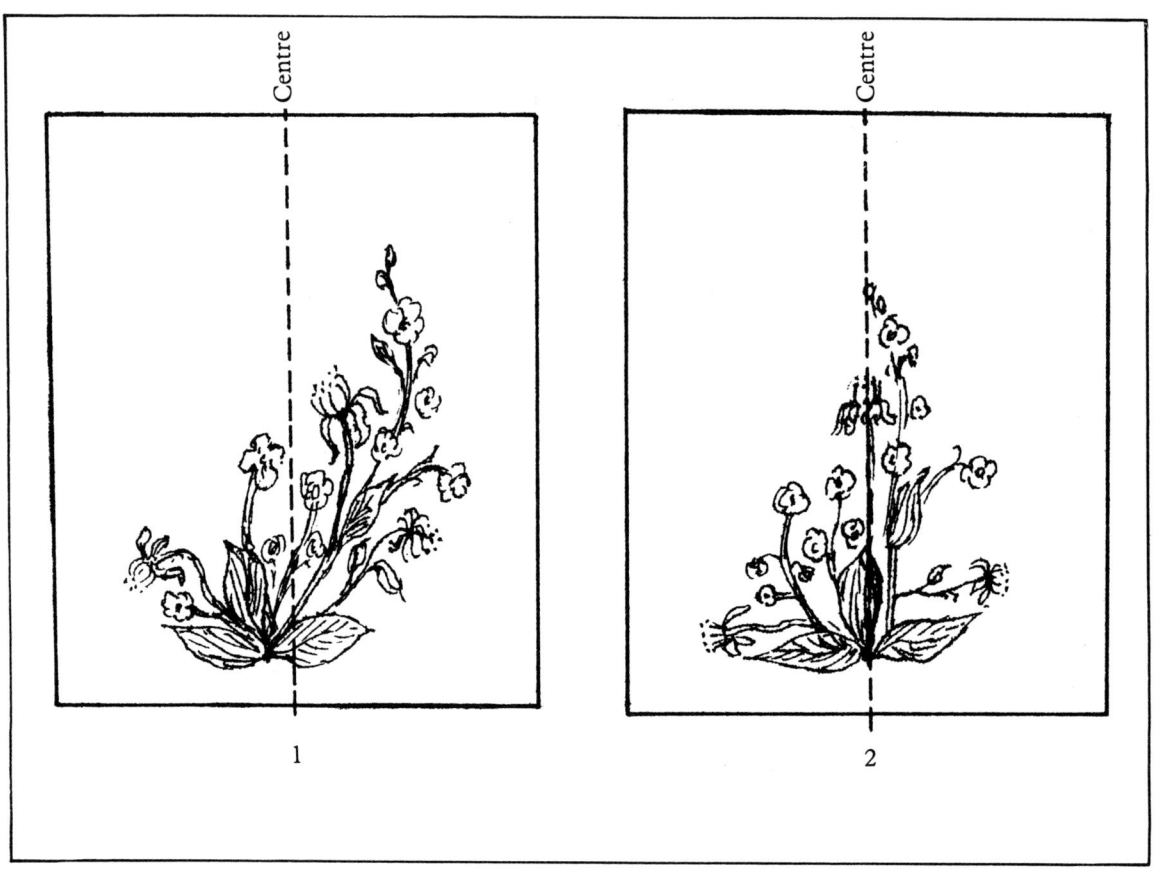

(vii) Flowers and stems can be used separately or attached. The gentle curve of stems enable the eye to follow through to a main feature, or give the natural link between leaves and flowers.

Background card
Greetings cards, calendars and texts

(viii) Avoid using white. Pastel coloured card purchased from stationers or art shops can be cut to the required size to make a firm background for calendars.

Deckle edged or plain thick notepaper saves preparation for greetings cards and texts. Notepaper in soft colours with matching envelopes adds to the uniqueness of greetings, get-well or thank you cards which you have made to give special pleasure to the recipient.

With God nothing shall be impossible. Buddleia, the darker variety, presses to deep purple which contrasts and links the candy tuft and silver leaves.

Cow parsley forms the central feature from which dogwood leaves, laburnum and cornflower florets flow in a simple design.

Made by using sheets of notepaper with a deckled edge and finally covering with contact or by lamination for protection, these texts are always popular for church bazaars.

Book marks and finger plates

When cutting card use a Stanley knife and metal guide, like a steel rule. This will give a clear cut whereas scissors may leave a jagged edge. Use a coloured card for these book marks approximately 22cm (9in) long by 5cm (2in) wide; make a mark at the centre point of the bottom line of the card. Now measure 2.5cm (1in) up on both sides, mark both points. Draw a diagonal line from each point at the sides to the centre mark at the bottom and this will give a point at the bottom base of the book mark if cut carefully with a Stanley knife and steel rule, or strip of metal. Finger plate card should be cut exactly to fit within the mould, place finger plate over the card and use a needle to mark the centre of the screw holes.

Pictures

Background card or material

If you have a suitable frame then the shape, size and colour of the background material should be considered against the type of frame to be used. If you have no frame readily available, select the colour of the background and choose the frame on completion of the picture.

Before you begin, check that your pressed materials to be used in the design look right on the background of your choice.

Background shapes

Rectangles are most suitable to begin with.

Ovals and circles are less versatile, requiring special attention to the flow of the shapes. Be sure you have a frame within which to work. Place this on your material and allow for an imaginary margin all round.

Squares are most suitable when the design radiates from an important central feature, often the largest flower or group of flowers forming a symmetrical design in ever-increasing circles. (*See symmetrical design: coloured plate 6*).

Choosing the colour of background material depends on:
(a) Pressed materials with which you intend making the picture;
(b) The type of frame available;
(c) The decor of the room in which it is to hang.

Dark colours are suitable for most large flowers, grasses and coloured leaves but are not recommended for delicate arrangements of tiny flowers. This is, however, a matter of personal choice. Pastel shades make pleasant, easy-to-work-on backgrounds, whereas bold backgrounds call for a bolder application.

Preparing the design

Having selected the base, look through the pressed flowers, leaves and grasses you have in mind to use. This is when you will be glad you labelled the contents of your press. Be careful to avoid exposing too much; only take out your immediate requirements. The longer your flowers are exposed to the air, the sooner they will deteriorate. Work in a dry atmosphere, keep windows closed on a damp day and avoid sudden draughts. To have prepared a design which is ruined by the opening of a door, closing of a book, or someone sneezing, is aggravating, especially if flowers are wafted on to the floor. Beware, too, of working whilst wearing a bracelet which dangles, or cuffs and sleeves which get in the way and have a tendency to 'collect' the flowers. A leaf or flower may mysteriously disappear; after seeking it everywhere that precious little scarlet pimpernel may well be clinging to your sleeve!

Now you are ready to place your flowers. Have a piece of card the same size as background material of picture. This will enable you to prepare your design and then transfer it piece by piece when you finally fix the flowers. Limit the selection of flowers to begin with, remember odd numbers, colour combination, shape variation and size variation.

Decide where the floral base and central features are to be placed (don't forget the margin), get this into position, work from there, tapering upwards, gently curving left or right, making sure the smaller of a group of three is furthest away from the base feature. Beginning with a base of three leaves forming a triangle is a good start – these may be feathery like pyrethrum leaves or cow parsley which may be broken into smaller leaves. Fumitory, and garden leaves of many types can be reduced in size; love-in-a-mist, larkspur, fennel, old man's beard, are all most useful link material. Small rose leaves – garden or wild – and blackberry in groups of three – as they grow – contrast well with daisy-type flowers. Try different shapes of leaves with your flower arrangement and finally choose one type only for your first attempt – remember AVOID the cluttered look.

Stinging nettle flowers are very useful 'links' which may often fill a gap and make the final touches to your design to emphasise direction. *Note:* Do not confuse these with dead-nettle flowers (see illustration).

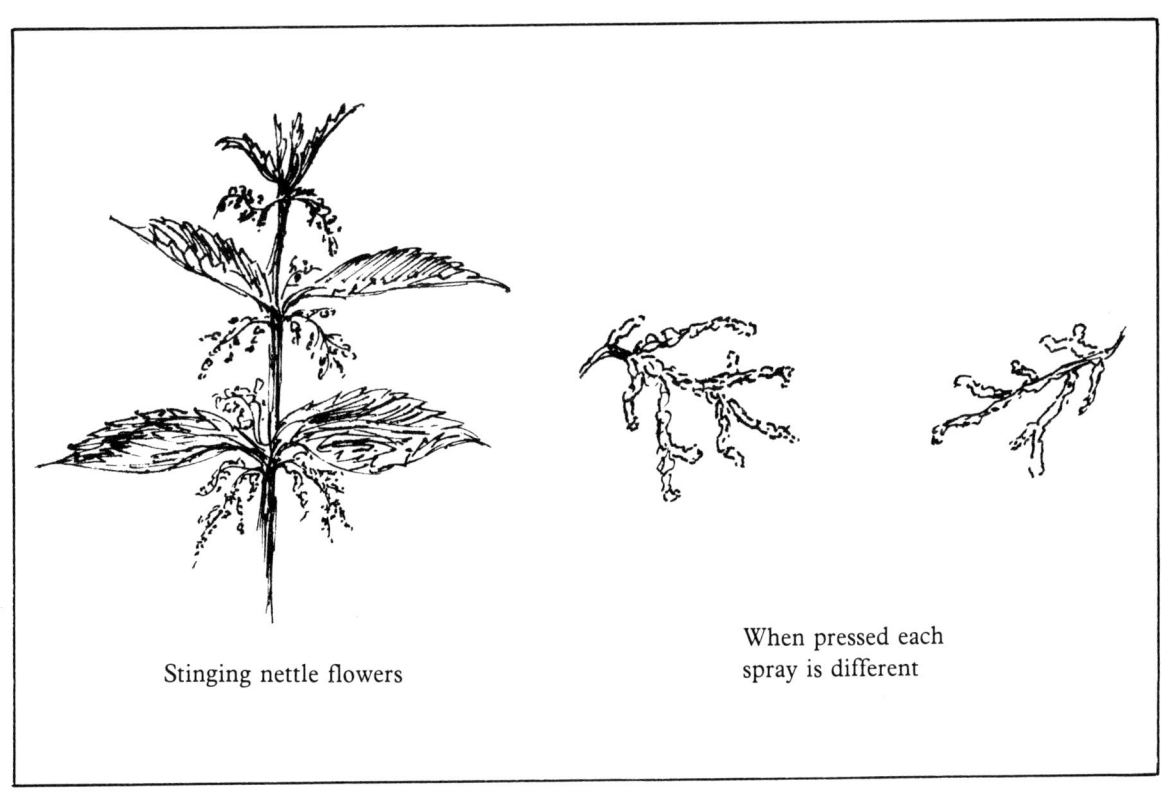

Stinging nettle flowers

When pressed each spray is different

Symmetrical design

This takes comparatively larger quantities of materials because as a design it either radiates in a circle or is based on a four-corner design. Flowers must be matched for shape, size and colour. This selection of matching and grading takes time and patience as it also applies to leaves and grasses, but the result can be pleasing, rewarding and satisfying to the designer.

In symmetrical designs even numbers of flowers, grasses and leaves will be used – 2, 4, 6, 8, etc, as well as groups of 3, 5 or 7, depending on the size of the design. A central feature adds to the interest and a variation at the top and bottom centre of the outside circle breaks the continuity and reduces the number of matched flowers – if you have difficulty in matching so many.

Circular design in a square frame

First find the centre of sides, top and bottom by measuring with a ruler, mark with a tiny pencil spot at the very edge of background material. Take the ruler, place on top and bottom spot and measure half way, make tiny spot. Do the same horizontally across the centre. Now you have the exact centre of the background. From the top centre measure down to allow for frame margin, this may be about 4cm (1½in). Do the same at sides and bottom, Mark with tiny spot. This gives a guide for outer circle. If you have a plate or saucer which just fits within this, it may be used to check that a perfect circle is formed as you place your flowers.

It is convenient to use various items such as saucers, plates and lids to get your decreasing circles. Determine each circle after first applying one quarter of the circle, as by this you will be able to see how far in the flowers will extend. Introduce leaves and grasses and work into the centre in this way. (*See coloured plate No. 6*).

It is helpful to design a quarter of the circle on a piece of card, or even the complete design, before finally transferring it to the background material or card for sticking.

A symmetrical design using a rectangle base

For this, measure inwards at sides, top and bottom 4cm (1½in) from edge at corners of material which has already been cut to size required for frame. Make four small pencil marks. These will be the four corners from which to work. Find the centre of the background material and mark it. If working on card, mark with feint pencil, if on material like satin, use tailor's chalk which can be brushed off if necessary, but it is possible that all tiny marks will be covered by the flowers or leaves. Work out the design on a sample card first before transferring and sticking to the background material or card. (*See coloured plate No. 7*).

Chapter 4

MINIATURES

Miniatures are fascinating to do, but tedious. The smallest flowers and leaves require skill and patience in preparing for pressing, and then fixing in a design without the trace of visible adhesive. I have placed this chapter later in the book because it was some years before I tackled the intricate art of handling such tiny flowers, pieces of leaves and smallest available grasses.

Picking

There are a number of tiny flowers which usually grow well-concealed amongst other flowers or very close to the ground. In my garden a tiny pink cranesbill, with small circular leaves hides in the edges of my lawn. Shepherd's-cress and hairy-bitter-cress grow amongst my roses offering tiny white flowers, and unusually shaped leaves. The tiny fairy flax, a low graceful slender plant with a white flower rather like a sandwort, grows on short downland turf amongst stronger plants like horseshoe vetch.

The flowers of bedstraw, yellow or white, are massed in large groups on a stem, sometimes twelve inches long. It is an eyecatching plant with strength of colour – as in the yellow which, when pressed will often turn to almost black; but whatever the result of your pressing you will find the tiny starlike flowers can be cut into groups and used to effect in miniatures.

Tiny leaves are essential; the illustrations of bitter-cress show the interesting grouping of leaves, which I find invaluable, tiny pieces of maidenhair fern, melilot, shamrock and clover leaves are ideal shapes. If you grow mind-your-own-business in a pot on the window sill, pick off the stems and you will notice how each one differs with tiny leaves

The blue cornflower florets, by their depth of blue and ragged petals, give a contrast to the solid shape of medick on slender stems and trail of melilot. This satin base has not been stuck to the card which forms a backing.

In the unframed miniature, wild thyme was chosen for the curve of the stem and tiny hair-like root attached. Mignonette are charming little shapes; though lacking in colour they add movement by resembling little children dancing. The pale mauve valerian have a hair-like stamen, if closely viewed. It is sometimes difficult to find suitable leaves for miniatures but by removing these tiny leaves from a stem of vetch and joining three at the base and three linking the mignonette this picture, 6cm x 5cm, holds a variety of interest which does not need the added grasses. Cover the grasses with your fingers and you will see what I mean.

growing at intervals which vary on each stem, in size and spacing. (*See illustrations*).

Delicate grasses – like bush grass, silver hair-grass and grey hair-grass can be quickly and easily picked in June and July, later to be cut into tiny groups after pressing.

Mommersteeg International Seed Breeders packet a variety of grasses which may be grown in pots or the garden to add to your collection of pressed materials, which will enhance miniature pictures if used in small quantities to add lightness of texture to an arrangement. Panicum violaceum and agrostis nebulosa-cloud grass are my recommendation for little pictures.

Ferns, which so often are grown in pots, make an excellent source of supply as small pieces may be nipped off the plant carefully from time to time, and pressed. Do not cut off too much greenery at one time – the plant will not only look sad, it may die.

Cut carefully with sharp scissors when picking, press immediately if you can, as these tinies will wilt quicky.

Lady's bedstraw

Pressing

The stems of such slender plants are easily placed into a gentle curve when preparing to press, and the little flowers may remain on the stems.

Separate each tiny flower on the head of thrift; they press beautifully with a sheen. Buddleia can be separated into groups of two or three flowers which usually turn out a deep purple. Bistort may not appear to be of any use, but it is possible to carefully separate each tiny pink or red flower from the head and press; they keep their colour very well. Elder flower, which contains a mass of tiny cream flowers and stamens, can be snipped off in groups of as many as eight, and press beautifully, later to be cut up individually as necessary. (*See illustration*).

Tiny clover leaf

Remove tiny flowers from main stems of alyssum (yellow or white), heaths, clover, vetch. With the greater knapweed, pull out side petals and press separately from the centre stamens. Carefully remove the tiny flowers of valerian, garlic and pink centaury. Yellow coridalis, melilot and horseshoe vetch should be pressed after removal from the stems: this is all very tedious and time consuming, but worth the effort if miniature pictures appeal to you. Looking for suitable flowers is most fascinating and often surprising.

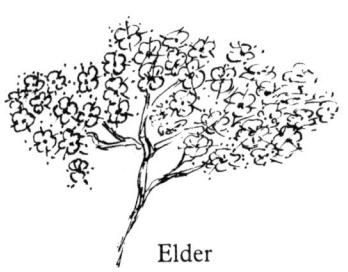

Elder

There are a variety of shrubs which offer heads of flowers, like veronicas, verbenas, spireas. Each tiny flower is snipped off and pressed separately but must be handled with great care to avoid damaging tiny stamens which add to their attractiveness.

Once you see the results of your first pressings, I am sure you will extend your searching beyond London pride, forget-me-nots, white

Wood forget-me-not

Small flowered cranesbill

Mind-your-own-business

Bitter-cress

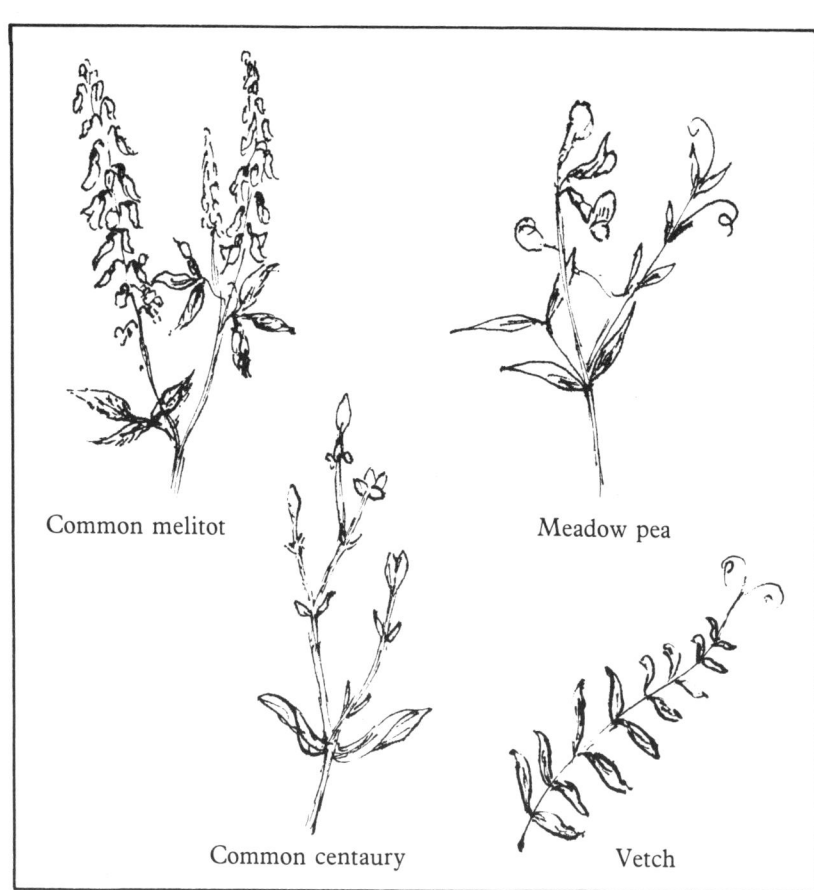

Common melitot

Meadow pea

Common centaury

Vetch

and yellow alyssums, and clovers. Ragged robin – the pink powder-puff mass found on wild roses – will press well when pulled apart.

Tiny leaves of bedstraw, bitter-cress and vetches press well between loo-paper, in fact, all very small leaves, whether green or red, are easier to handle when pressed this way.

When you start looking for tinies to press there is much to be found in window box, garden path, wall crevice, rockery or hedgerow.

Design

The principles are the same as for larger pictures: using a pin or darning needle, place your flowers with the minutest amount of adhesive, keeping your arrangement as dainty as possible, substituting tiny grasses for leaves, because of the delicacy of size and colouring, a mass of flowers rather than a 'growing' group is most effective, especially if mounted on a pastel background; it seems to throw up the colour. White flowers alyssum, fairyflax; and yellows – alyssum and melilot, always stand out clearly on grey. My miniatures are usually about 6cm x 4cm. If using a slightly larger base, there will obviously be a wider selection of flowers suitable.

Chapter 5

CANADIAN AND AUSTRALIAN PICTURES

As I had the pleasure of picking garden plants and so-called weeds in both countries, I thought that for the benefit of those readers living in Canada and Australia, I would add an appropriate picture.

Canada

The leaves pressed in 'the fall' surpass ours for shape and colour. I have nothing in my press to compare with those used on coloured plate 12 for variety in toning colour; added to these are the petals of zinnias, which may be used with or without the developing seed at the base of the petal. After loosening the petals of zinnias by rolling the calyx between finger and thumb; these I found pressed well separately, and used inside-out in a picture gave a light green shiny appearance, which could take the place of small leaves. The rose petals that I pressed in Canada kept their colours remarkably well; in fact, I had no failures, which may have been due to the dry weather conditions in Ontario at that time. Of course, I kept to the rule of picking after the sun had dried surplus moisture – about 11 am – and I did not pick late in the day if the sun had been on them most of the time. If the rule is remembered about picking flowers which are free from moisture on their petals, and not over exposed to the sun, the pressed results with pansies, salvias, daisies, alyssum, in fact most garden flowers, should be very satisfactory. Regrettably, the brilliant colour of geraniums is disappointing as they may not fade under press but do so quickly when used for a picture.

The blue chicory growing by the roadside delighted me as I rarely see it here, but I refrained from picking as I was certain it would fade in pressing, but I may well have been wrong.

Australia

How wonderfully bougainvillea keeps it colour of magenta, pink, red or orange bracts. In this picture shown on the previous page, you may notice that some have been pressed, some not, as I liked the interest which a slight crinkling gives. When I last visited Australia, it was around Adelaide that I gathered these few flowers, the little brown starlike flowers grow on any odd patch of ground. These were by the roadside and charmed me by their delicate petals with a brown centre stripe. The pale mauve and blue flowers were growing wild some miles from the city, and I persuaded my driver to stop and let me pick them. At that time I had no thought of writing a book, and they are, therefore, nameless, but they have retained their colour so well in spite of being kept a number of years. A yellow flower which delighted me grew prolifically in our garden, and sucking the stem of this was most refreshing; classed as a weed, the flower is a brilliant yellow, presses well and holds its colour. It is called Bermuda buttercup in England where it also blooms. Australian readers will no doubt identify it by another name. The books of Australian wild flowers which I have do not include the specimens used in the picture, so I am unable to give the names.

One day in the not too distant future, I should like to experiment with a variety of Australian flora of common varieties; I am sure pressing would be rewarding. However, as I mentioned under Canada, geraniums do quickly lose their wonderful colour once out of the press. This is unfortunate as I know they flourish in gardens and streets around South Australia, and no doubt in other states.

If you have not yet tried pressing sea-weed, I do commend it to you, as Australian sea-weed is not only very clean but the colours are excellent. First, when you get it home, wash it well a number of times in clear water, float it on a plate in a centimetre of water or less, slide blotting paper beneath it and remove whilst still floating by lifting the paper to enable the sea-weed to retain its natural shape. Allow the

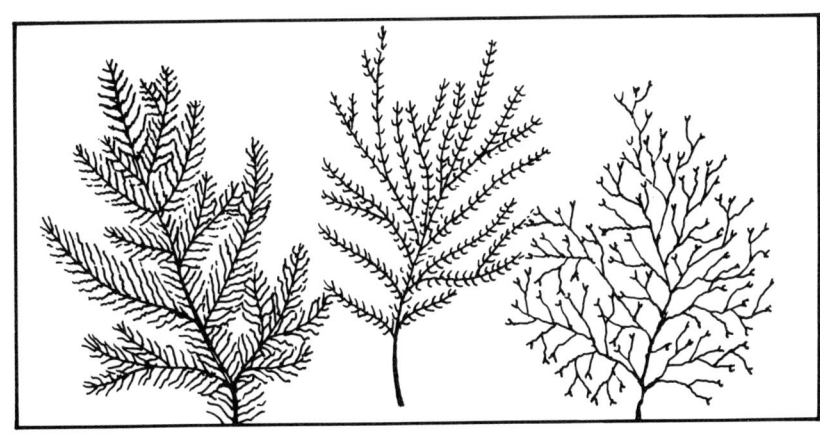

Opposite top:
This selection shows various ways in which a few flowers and leaves may be arranged to create pretty get-well, greetings, thank you, birthday cards or calendars using wild and garden flowers. In the right-hand picture phlox and the orange stamens of French marigold have been used. On the blue card the yellow stamens of the pink and red rock roses show up to advantage.

blotting paper to almost dry out and then press the sea-weed between four layers. The result is a charming lacy pattern. When ready to use, remove it very carefully with a needle eased between the sea-weed and blotting paper. No doubt, you will wish you had four hands – ask someone to help you by using another needle to keep it flat before placing it on to your picture background material. Make it a central feature and dot flowers around in the spaces to enhance the natural intricate pattern. It is possible to use sea-weed in smaller portions in place of leaves in a design, but do be certain you are in the right mood, as sticking so many tiny thread-like pieces requires time and patience. When you set it in place, lift small pieces at a time with a needle and carefully pass another needle, which is thinly coated in adhesive, beneath it. It should then adhere to the base without cockling or losing its shape.

Opposite bottom:
It is necessary to cover book marks with contact or have them laminated for protection. The gay buttercups and stinging nettle flowers, daisies and mind-your-own-business, candytuft and flowers of the plumbago shrub, all give pleasant reminders of summer days.

Plate 1

Below: Plate 2

Chapter 6

FIXING PRESSED MATERIALS

You will need
Blotting paper
Stanley knife
Steel rule
Cutting board
Pins and needles
Pencil
Scissors (large and tiny)
Darning needle
Two cocktail sticks
Tweezers
Adhesive
Paint brush
Pennies

As previously mentioned, various materials may be used as backgrounds for designs, and PVA adhesive for fixing. A sheet of blotting paper will protect the table.

Type of mounting
Card purchased from art shops or good stationers, can be obtained in large sheets of various colours and thicknesses and will cut into shapes and sizes as required, the off-cuts left are useful for book marks or greetings cards. Measure carefully to get the size required for a picture, draw the exact size to fit the frame if you already have one,

allowing about one millimetre less than exact inset of frame all round. Place the card to be cut on a surface which will not be damaged by the Stanley knife blade – a chopping board is excellent. Place the steel rule or any metal strip along the pencil outlines and cut through clean with Stanley knife. If scissors are used, the card may be damaged and edges 'chewed'.

Card is a firm background and adhesive will not penetrate, but the adhesive must be used sparingly. Place a small quantity on a jam jar lid and leave it a few minutes before using it. Now very carefully pick up the first leaf or flower, either with your fingers or tweezers, turn it over away from the dummy background (and final background) and apply the PVA by using a cocktail stick or darning needle, which has been dipped into the lid gently to avoid a big blob of PVA forming. When this is applied to the back of the flower be sure to place it either on sepals – little pieces of green at the back of the flower – or on the stem. If the flower is like montbretia, removed from any sepals, place the adhesive at the base of the flower where a double thickness may be found. Now gently lift flower, reverse it and place on the picture background. Apply a slight pressure with your finger on the surface to make certain the flower is secured.

Begin by fixing the bottom of your design in the correct position as this will enable the work to progress upwards and it is easier to make any adjustments to your design if you can establish the centre focal point to which all else relates. (*See plate 9*). It may be that you have designed a diagonal spray; if so, begin by fixing the central feature of that first, and work outwards in both directions. Always remember that tiny pieces of grasses can be added as final touches to link flowers or extend the design in any desirable direction to give lightness and movement.

One of my first disasters was the result of putting adhesive on the delicate petals of rockrose and primrose. When the adhesive dried out the petals had shrunk with it and finished up a crinkly mess. I also made the mistake of putting too much adhesive behind the flowers, as in the case of a little daisy. When put on the card and pressed with my finger, the adhesive oozed out, on to my fingers, onto the petals and the card. When it dried the result was a shiny surface on the card around the flowers, crinkly petals on the daisy and a spot on the card because I did not realise I had PVA on my finger! If, however, the flowers and leaves need to be firmly fixed, as in the case of a greetings card, then gently lift the petals of a flower (another cocktail stick may help) and allow the PVA on the cocktail stick or needle to touch the edge of the petal with the minutest spot, and press the petal on the card with a finger, keeping it quite smooth. This will come with practice and requires delicacy of touch.

As you apply adhesive to leaves, notice the main vein at the base; this can be the fixing point; put it on the card where required, press

Overleaf:
Cornflowers, which are perennial cultivated plants often regarded as weeds, are an asset to the pressed flower craft enthusiast. In this picture it shows how each flower section can be reassembled to make an interesting circular motif or used in smaller groups giving a spiky effect in contrast to the shapes of the autumn leaves. In this picture only two colours have been used.

Opposite: Plate 3

Plate 4

Below: Plate 5

Previous Page top:
Rectangle
Dogwood leaves, light blue larkspur, stamens and florets of cornflower form an attractive arrangement with a byrony tendril to suggest movement.

Circular
Columbines and leaves of traveller's joy (old man's beard) make an unusual combination of shape and colour. The grasses link and add daintiness. Columbines used in this picture were pressed face-down complete, the spurs were then pressed down with the finger to the positions shown in the picture.

Previous Page bottom:
Feathers give a flyaway lightness and add a brighter shade of green with touches of white to this picture of oak and sumach leaves. Small contrasting leaves placed at the base of the larger leaves not only add interest but give the effect of reducing the size of the base leaves.

White rose petals turn to a shade of honey with darker veining when pressed and these have been assembled to form simple flowers. The bold colour of autumn leaves give contrast to the flowers of delicate lacey hedge parsley (Queen Anne's lace).

gently with your finger, allow a minute or two before gently raising and touching with the adhesive at its points. By experience it will become easy to recognise the most important parts of a leaf or flower which should have an extra touch of adhesive to avoid damage to a greetings card through handling by the recipient.

Work through the fixing of the design; now incorporate a few pieces of grass if you have made a number of satisfactory arrangements.

When grasses are picked and pressed it is usually with a main stalk holding masses of tiny stems and small heads. The stems are almost hair-like, but very strong and wiry. Snip a number of these off the main stem, use them to add lightness by fixing the bases of tiny stems first. Run your adhesive up the stem while holding the head in your fingers. Place the stem in position where required and immediately put a penny on it. This will fix it in a few minutes, then lift the small head of the grass, lightly pass your adhesive behind it and with the greatest care, using another cocktail stick, needle or pin, direct the head to where it is required to stick, and place another penny on it. It is tedious, but so worth while. A little practice and you will find it possible to make the grasses curve to your requirements which will enhance a picture by the effect of movement. (*See plates 4 and 10*).

Velvet. The pile makes sticking difficult but it is possible to follow the instructions as for card, but check that sufficient adhesive is used to hold the flowers in place without putting any at all on the petals, as this would be for framing and glazing only.

Bolder grasses are easier to use on velvet than the delicate type, and leaves can be very effective.

The enthusiast will naturally want to meet the challenge of various background materials, however difficult.

Providing the pile is close, it is possible to use velvet as a background for a picture which is to be framed but, remembering glass is to cover it, the effect of the pile is lost in the pressure of framing and becomes unrecognisable as velvet. Added to this is the difficulty of sticking the flowers to a surface which tends to have slight movement as you apply flowers. Personal experience of disappointment when my velvet based pictures were framed prevents me from advocating its use. However, use the same method to measure as for card, but cut carefully with scissors.

Another method I have used is to cut a piece of cardboard to the size required, spread PVA adhesive completely over the card and wait for it to dry off. When dry it takes on the appearance of being 'shiny'. Take your piece of velvet, and lay this on the prepared surface of the cardboard. Place a piece of brown paper over the top of the material and, using a hot iron, press over the covered area. When the material has stuck, trim it with a pair of scissors. From personal experience I have found that quite often air bubbles appear on the material and it is

Using velvet as a background

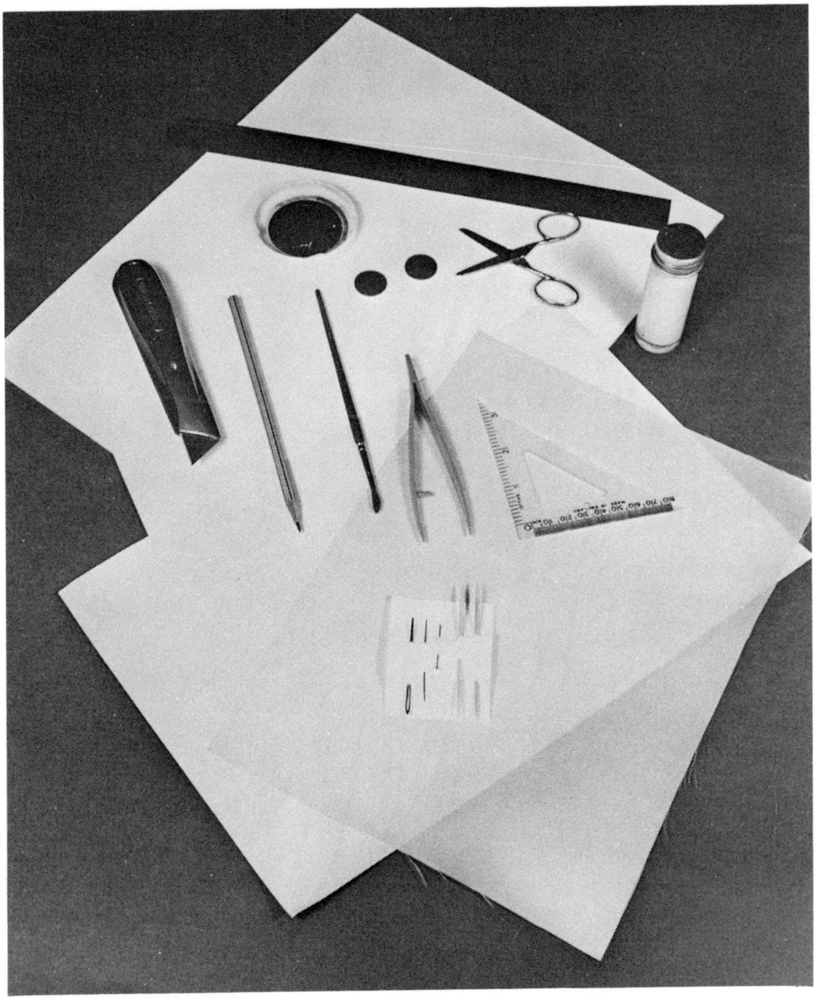

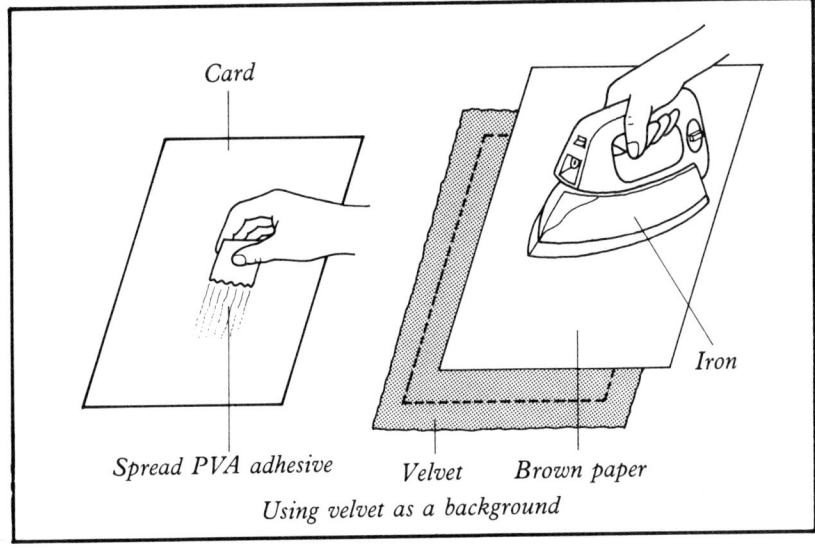

Overleaf:
A symmetrical design on satin which could be framed in a moulding to give a rectangular shape, or in an oval frame. At the top of the design is a piece of Queen Anne's lace and two small flowered cranesbill leaves and elder flowers, which is repeated at the base and sides but without the elder flowers. Heartsease and bistort flowers form the rest of the outer circle. The groups of bistort flowers are linked by forget-me-nots around a centre of Queen Anne's lace and a yellow loosestrife.

Opposite: Plate 6

Plate 7

Below: Plate 8

Previous Page top:
The simple rectangular pattern on satin is a combination of wild flowers. The four dandelions are linked by gorse, and the tiny sprays of mind-your-own-business with grasses direct the eye to a centre circle of tiny cultivated red bistort flowers around a daisy.

Previous Page bottom:
The golden Hypericum also known as St John's wort or rose of Sharon, deep blue delphiniums, purple lavendar pieces and anchusa flowers are softened by a background of rhus which also links the complete arrangement. The stamens of rose of Sharon can be pressed separately and used as centres for other flowers.

impossible to get rid of them. So this method is not recommended for satin or Tricel.

Satin or Tricel. Either of these materials are quite suitable for more advanced students. Press with a warm iron to remove the slightest wrinkle, measure the size as for card but cut carefully with large scissors. Take great care not to fray the satin.

The sheet of blotting paper used as a working base under satin or Tricel is important, as the adhesive will go through these materials marking the surface of the table on which you work, and you could find you have a picture firmly fixed to it! With blotting paper, the satin is less slippery; it is also firmer than paper and if you lift the satin from time to time and move it carefully to a fresh place, the adhesive which may have seeped through will not fix your picture securely to it.

Chapter 7

FRAMING

My first pictures were designed on card to fit frames from which old photographs had been removed. When I had exhausted my supply, I made use of rummage sales, charity and antique shops; friends, too, joined the hunt and in this way I built up a selection of sizes and shapes which, after stripping down and cleaning, sometimes required touching up.

Wooden frames

When the frame is ready to use place the clean glass in position on top of your picture, turn it over and place in frame, face down. Cover this with another piece of thick card or hardboard according to the depth of the inside frame edge. Using panel pins gently tap in diagonally one pin in each left-hand corner of frame, propping the frame firmly against a supporting ridge. Check that the picture is in place correctly – no petals bent under. Now fix further pins in the centre and right-hand corners by turning the frame around to allow the small hammer to drive pins in diagonally. Cut a sheet of brown paper to the size of the back of frame and picture; paste over with wallpaper paste and allow to dry. Repeat this and place on the entire back to the edge of the frame. If it is slightly over size, then trim by resting the rule firmly just within the edge of the frame and cutting firmly through; providing the paper is still damp it will cut through cleanly.

Purchased moulding

It is possible to purchase moulding of your choice and have it cut to your own requirements at do-it-yourself shops; be sure to give the exact measurements of your picture. With an angle aid you can fix

Overleaf:
This is a very simple picture of leaves and grasses. It takes longer and is more difficult to plan and assemble than a picture massed with flowers but the use of grasses is always a challenge which is worth pursuing and the results can be most interesting.

59

Opposite: Plate 9

Plate 10

Below: Plate 11

Previous Page top: Small pieces of pink candytuft flowers with daisies, buttercups, cow parsely and stinging-nettle flowers show up boldly in two circular pictures complementing the more delicate arrangement of muted shades blending with the single begonia. Although begonias lose their colour under press the shape is unusual with a predominant little centre of cream stamens.

Previous Page bottom: Double red May flowers, 'keys' of the ash tree used separately in place of leaves, and hedge parsley make an interesting combination on a blue background.

The larger oval frame is a heavier type which requires a bolder arrangement, The blue larkspur is linked by dogwood leaves which are nicely veined, and the fuchsia has the stamens placed to form a pleasing group. Three flowers of traveller's joy (old man's beard) have silvery centres. These were picked in July when the flowers were a creamy colour before the silvery centre became fluffy.

Willowherb, dead-nettle and rhus has been used in this picture to give a delicate contrast to the three primulas.

your frame together by first sticking the mitred ends with a wood adhesive. Then proceed as before, with glass purchased to the size of your picture.

Circular and oval frames

These are available to purchase in art and DIY shops and will invariably require glass cut to size. Metal and plastic frames are usually sold complete with glass.

Laminating

This is a process whereby the picture is passed through two rollers of plastic and with heat and pressure covers the picture, eliminating air and preserving the flowers. Before making a picture which is to be covered in this way, check with the laminating operator that the card thickness is suitable – velvet or satin does not laminate satisfactorily. It is recommended for calendars or pictures on card to be framed without glass. Unfortunately I have not yet found a way of writing on this surface; therefore, greetings or get-well cards can be covered only with a thin clear 'contact' which is adhesive on one side. This is cut to size before removing its protective covering, place the top edge to the card after exposing an inch of adhesive surface. As you press this down, gradually remove the protective covering, pressing as you go, round the flowers and leaves as closely as possible. Carefully trim off any overlap.

Glazing

When purchasing glass to fit a frame you have acquired, bought or made, there are two alternatives – plain or non-reflective. Using non-reflective gives an interesting effect as all reflections are eliminated and light is deflected which helps the preservation of colour, but at the same time there is a very slight green tinge to the glass which alters the overall effect. This is hardly noticeable and only the most discerning eye detects it.

Plain glass gives a sharper effect, does not deflect the light and the reflections are unavoidable.

Different people, different tastes. I find non-reflective is more expensive. Try the pictures you make under both types of glass and make your personal choice.

Chapter 8

GROW YOUR OWN WILD FLOWERS
By C. J. Hambidge of Mr Fothergill's Seeds

Wild flowers are on the decline. Even those we regard as common, poppies and cowslips for example, are rapidly disappearing and will continue to do so unless efforts are made to save them. Many have to adapt to changing environments in order to survive, and those that cannot are being edged out of existence. The easiest way to save such flowers is to grow them from seed, and one company, Mr Fothergill's Seeds, of Kentford, Suffolk, offers the seed of twenty-four of our best loved varieties, several now very rare. A large rural garden is not necessary to appreciate the beauty and charm of these flowers which can be grown even where space is severely limited.

Primrose, cowslip and violet are all suitable as pot-plants, and as they are perennial they will flower year after year. With these three varieties germination can often be improved if the seed is pre-chilled prior to sowing, although it is not absolutely essential. Pre-chilling the seeds for a few weeks simulates the effect of winter which they would undergo in their natural habitat. All this entails is mixing the seed with a little damp sand, sealing it in a polythene bag and putting it in a refrigerator. It is more satisfying to be able to grow pot-plants from seed than to buy them from a nurseryman whose prices can be high. It is now difficult to find any quantity of these varieties growing wild, and so anyone wishing to grow them from seed enjoys the added satisfaction of producing something rare and endangered.

Nowadays, there is an increasingly large number of people without a garden or, at most, a tiny one. For those who live in flats, a window-sill or balcony has to double as a garden, but there is still a surprising variety of plants that can be grown in such situations. Two more perennials, Cheddar pink and maiden pink, are ideal in window-boxes and tubs. Cheddar pink is now so rare in this country (it grows wild

Opposite: Plate 12
The shape, veining and colour of Canadian autumn leaves are used in this picture to form a simple spray with flowers made of zinnia petals.

only on Cheddar Gorge) that it is protected by Act of Parliament. They are as easy to grow as cultivated pinks. Wild pansy or heartsease is another excellent subject in a window-box. This is an annual, and such flowers are the easiest of all to grow, sowing them either the autumn before or the spring of the year in which they are to flower. Heartsease is a much more delicate flower than its garden cousins, its petals ranging in colour from cream to deep purple. Thrift, too, makes a grand display and was once a cottage garden favourite. Generally associated with coastal areas, this short, neat perennial is at home in window-boxes.

Pasqueflower, traditionally said to flower at Easter, looks almost too exotic to be a native British flower – but it is! Its soft purple petals and yellow eye make an arresting centre-piece in a tub or urn.

Hanging baskets are now immensely popular, and wild flowers can even be made to feel at home in these. Lady's finger, which tends to trail, can look every bit as effective as trailing lobelia or petunia, and, along with another perennial, toadflax, can make a delightful show, often when other flowers are getting past their best.

The introduction in recent years of growing bags has opened up new horizons for those of us whose space is severely limited. While most people tend to buy them for the production of tomatoes and cucumbers, they can also be used effectively on a balcony or patio as a miniature wild flower garden. Their scope is endless. Imagine being able to grow foxgloves on a balcony! Growing bags enable you to do just that. Annuals such as poppy, ox-eye daisy, pheasant's eye, cornflower, corn cockle and corn marigold are all that are needed to give a show all summer long in a growing bag.

The countryside can now be taken anywhere, and in an age when life is increasingly centred in towns and cities it is a reassuring thought. Wild flowers are now greatly at risk, and it is only through enthusiasm and perseverence that we will be able to ensure their safety. It is a process in which we can all play a part.

Chapter 9

PICKING AND PRESSING THROUGH THE SEASONS

Throughout the year there is always something to press. Shrubs bloom at various times and these have not been included in the list, but are worthy of experimentation: simply remove individual flowers for pressing; many leaves of shrubs are suitable if interesting in shape and colour.

The following list of flowers, both wild and cultivated, are mainly common. Of course, it could be very extensive, but it is intended as a guide to the presser month by month. Obviously, plants which bloom in the early summer are often found blooming later in the season, and this varies in different areas of the country.

I am often asked to give a list of flowers which retain their colour when pressed. There can be no hard and fast answer to this question as so much depends on weather conditions and even the time of day. Avoid picking after rain and morning dew, allow sufficient time for flowers to be free of surface moisture, but remember that too much sun means the flowers are not fresh. Take into account the seasons and age of the flower when picked.

The Wild Plants Act of 1975 states that no person, unless authorised, or with reasonable excuse, may uproot any wild plant.

Useful addresses

Mr Fothergill's Seeds, Regal Lodge, Gazeley Road, Kentford, Newmarket, Suffolk CB8 7QB.

Mommersteeg International, Station Road, Finedon, Wellingborough, Northants NN9 5NT.

Suttons Seeds Ltd, Hele Road, Shiphay, Torquay, Devon.

W. J. Unwin Ltd, Histon, Cambridge CB4 4LE.

Key to abbreviations
c = *Cultivated*
F = *Obtainable in seed packets from Mr Fothergill's Seeds*
MI = *Obtainable in seed packets from Mommersteeg International*
pw = *Presses well*

Month	**Plant**	**Colour**		
January	Aconite (Winter)	yellow		The only yellow spring flower with a sepal-like green frill or ruff. Blooms Jan-Mar.
	Blackberry Leaves	dark maroon silver underside	pw	These may be found during winter months, very useful.
	Dead Nettle	pale or dark pinkish purple		Blooms throughout the year.
	Heliotrope	lilac		Blooms Nov-Mar. The leaves are round and downy.
	Jasmine (Winter)	yellow	c pw	Blooms Nov-Mar. Leaves and flowers, but must be quite dry.

February	Coltsfoot	yellow	pw	Feb-Apr.
	Crocus	yellow and purple	c pw	Cut in half to press.
	Gorse	yellow	pw	Blooms throughout the year – only sparsely in Jan and Feb.
	Heaths	various	c	Blooms throughout the year.
	Hellebore	green or deep maroon	c	Press flower complete.
	Primrose	sulphur yellow	F MI pw	Feb-May.
	Snowdrop	white	c pw	Remove flower and press face down.
	Violet (Sweet)	deep violet	F MI	Pressing results unreliable.

Month	Plant	Colour		
March	Aubrieta	mauves	*c*	Mar-Apr. Press, turning to white or partly mauve.
	Anemone	deep blue, red, white	*c* *pw*	Press petals.
	Arabis	pink, white	*c* *pw*	Mar-May. Press on stem.
	Bermuda Buttercup	yellow	*pw*	Mar-Jun. Scilly Isles.
	Celandine	yellow		Mar-May. Fades to white eventually.
	Daffodil	yellow	*c*	Remove from calyx and press after cutting in half.
	Marsh Marigold	yellow		Press flowers only.
	Oxlip	yellow	*MI*	Mar-May. Similar to cowslip. Found in Suffolk, Essex, Cambs and Beds.
	Primula	various	*c*	Mar-May.
	Violet (Wood Dog)	pale violet		Variable pressing results.
	White Dead-Nettle	white		Presses to cream flower.
	Wood Anemone	white		Wilts quickly.

April	Alyssum	yellow	*c*	Press on stem.
	Black Medick	yellow		Trefoil leaves, press separately.
	Bluebell	blue		Variable pressing results.
	Campion	red		Remove flowers from calyx.
	Cowslip	yellow	*F* *MI*	Invariably turn green when pressed.
	Cow Parsley	white	*pw*	Press head complete or separately.

Month	Plant	Colour		
	Dandelion	yellow	*pw*	Press flowers and leaves separately.
	Forget-me-not	blue	*MI* *F*	Press on stem or separately.
	Gentian (Spring)	blue	*MI* *pw*	Apr-Jun.
	Grape Hyacinth	blue	*c*	Press complete after first removing flowers from one side.
	Heartsease (Wild Pansy)	violet, white and yellow	*F* *MI* *pw*	Apr-Sept.
	Lady's Smock	deep lilac to white	*pw*	Apr-Jun. Press flowers and stems complete.
	Milkwort (Chalk)	gentian blue, pink or white	*pw*	Apr-Jun. Press complete.
	Pasque Flower	violet	*F*	Apr-May. Press flowers separately.
	Polyanthus	various	*c*	Press flowers separately.
	Stitchwort (Greater)	white	*pw*	Press complete.
	Tulip	red, yellow	*c*	Press petals separately.

May	Birds-foot Trefoil	yellow, orange	*MI*	May-Sept. Sometimes turns green when pressed.
	Broom	yellow		May-June. Press flowers only.
	Bryony (White)	yellowish green		May-Sept. Press tendrils and flowers.
	Buttercup	yellow	*pw*	May onwards.
	Campion	white		May onwards. Press flower and calyx.
	Cheiranthus	orange	*c* *pw*	Press flowers separately.
	Clover	red		May onwards. Press complete or individually.
	Cranesbill	deep violet-blue	*MI*	May-Sept. Press leaves and flowers on stem or separately.

Month	Plant	Colour		
	Fairy Flax	white		May onwards. Press complete.
	Fumitory	pinkish-purple		May-June.
	Gentian	blue	*MI*	May onwards.
	Hop Trefoil	yellow	*pw*	Press separately.
	Horseshoe Vetch	deep yellow	*pw*	Press complete head of flowers.
	Lady's Finger		*F*	May onwards. Press separately.
	Lawn Daisy	white	*pw*	Press flowers.
	London Pride	pale pink	*c pw*	Press flowers on stems.
	Ox-Eye Daisy	white	*F MI*	May onwards.
	Pimpernel	scarlet	*MI*	May-Nov.
	Poppy (Field)	scarlet	*MI*	Petals are very delicate when pressed.
	Pulsatilla	mauve	*c pw*	The feathery seed heads.
	Pyrethrum	red, pink, white	*c*	Press flower petals and leaves.
	Silverweed	yellow flower, silver leaf	*pw*	May-Aug. Leaves.
	Sweet William	red, pink, white	*c*	May-July. Press flowers only.
	Thrift	pink	*F*	May onwards. Separate flowers to press
	Wallflowers	pink, orange, red, yellow	*c*	Press flowers only.
	Wild Radish	white petals, lilac veined		Press with stems.
	Yarrow	white, pink	*MI*	Press leaves. Flowers are bulky.
June	Anchusa	blue	*c*	Press flowers only.
	Bitter-cress	white		June-Aug.
	Bladder Campion	white		June-Aug.
	Chamomile	white	*F*	June-Aug. Press leaves and flowers separately.

Month	Plant	Colour		
	Cheddar Pink	pink	F	June-July.
	Chives	pink		Separate flowers to press.
	Cinquefoil	yellow	pw	Flowers and leaves press well.
	Common Centaury	pink		June onwards.
	Corncockle	red	F	June-Aug.
	Cornflower (perennial)	blue		Retains colour if separated for pressing.
	Cornflower (wild)	blue	F	June-Aug.
	Corn Marigold	yellow	F	June onwards.
	Corn Poppy	red	F	June onwards.
	Corydalis	yellow	pw	June onwards.
	Delphinium	blue, white	c pw	Press flowers complete,
	Elder	cream	pw	June – short season.
	Flax (perennial)	blue	F	June-July.
	Foxglove	pinkish purple	F	June-Sept. Not attractive when pressed.
	Hawkbit	yellow		June onwards.
	Hawksbeard	yellow		June onwards.
	Hawkweed	yellow		June onwards.
	Hogweed	white		Cream when pressed.
	Honeysuckle	cream deepening to orange-buff	pw	June-Sept. Separately.
	Lesser Stitchwort	white		Press on stems.
	Maiden Pink	pink	F pw	June-Aug.
	Mallow	pinkish-purple		Press flowers.
	Mayweed	white		June-Aug.
	Melilot	yellow	pw	Press complete or each flower separately.
	Nemesia	various	c pw	Press flowers separately.
	Pansy	deep maroon, yellow	c pw	June onwards.
	Pheasant's Eye	scarlet	F	June onwards.

Month	Plant	Colour		
	Poppy (Shirley)	orange yellow	*pw*	Press petals.
	Poppy (Welsh)	yellow	*F*	June-Aug.
	Ragwort	yellow		June onwards. Interesting to press buds also.
	Rose	various	*c*	Press petals separately.
	Rose of Sharon	yellow	*pw*	June onwards.
	Scabious (Field)	bluish-lilac		June onwards.
	Stinging Nettle	catkins of tiny greenish flowers	*pw*	June onwards.
	Stonecrop	white or pink		Press individual flowers.
	Wild Mignonette	greenish yellow		June onwards. Press each flower separately.
	Wild Thyme	reddish purple		June-Aug. Press complete.

July	Achillea	yellow	*c* *pw*	Press each tiny flower separately.
	Alyssum	white, mauve	*c* *pw*	Press on stem or separately for miniatures.
	Asters	various	*c*	Press petals separately.
	Bedstraw	white		July-Aug.
	Bedstraw (Lady's)	yellow	*MI*	Jul-Sept.
	Buddleia	mauve	*c*	Deep purple when pressed singly.
	Candytuft	pink, mauve, white	*c* *pw*	Jul-Aug. Press individual flowers, not the complete head.
	Fennel	yellow		Press flowers and greenery separately.
	Feverfew	white	*MI*	Press flowers and leaves separately.
	Geranium	scarlet	*c*	Press flowers complete, results are variable.
	Greater Knapweed	purple		Pull apart to press.
	Harebell	blue	*F*	Not recommended for pressing. July onwards.

Month	Plant	Colour		
	Larkspur	pink, red, blue, white	c pw	Jul-Sept. Flowers and foliage separately.
	Lobelia	blue, white	c pw	Press on stem.
	Marjoram	pale mauve		Jul-Sept.
	Montbretia	orange	c	Jul-Aug. Excellent pressed on stem or separately.
	Phlox	pink, mauve, white	c	Jul-Aug.
	Rosebay (Willowherb)	pink	pw	Press flowers only.
	Scabious (small)	pale mauve		Now always successful.
	Spiked Speedwell	blue	F pw	July onwards.
	St John's Wort	yellow	F pw	July onwards.
	Targetes	orange, yellow	c	Press flower complete or separately.
	Toadflax	yellow	pw	To press remove flowers from calyx.
	Willowherb	pink	pw	Press the head to include the seed pods.

Month	Plant	Colour		
August	Dahlia	various	c	Aug-Nov. Press petals separately.
	Fuchsia	various pinks, reds, whites	c pw	Cut in half to press.
	Gaillardia	yellow-scarlet	c pw	Aug-Sept. Press petals only.
	Golden Rod	yellow	c pw	Aug-Sept. Press in small sprays.
	Helenium	yellow, orange	c	Aug-Sept. Press petals only.
	Marigold (Calendula)	orange, yellow	c pw	Press petals separately or complete.
	Marigold (French)	yellow to deep orange	c pw	Aug-Oct. Press petals only.
	Mugwort			The leaves of this plant are worthy of note if reversed.

Month	Plant	Colour		
	Salvia	scarlet	c pw	Separate flower to press.
	Zinnia	various	c pw	Press petals separately.

September	Chrysan- themum	various	c	Sept-Nov. Press petals separately.
	Lawn Daisy	white		Sept-Oct. Last seasons picking.
	Michaelmas Daisy	pink, mauve	c	Press flowers.
	Rudbeckia	deep yellow	c pw	Sept onwards. Press petals.
	Sunflowers (various types)	yellow	c pw	Sept-Oct. Press petals separately.
	Thistle			Press the down before it blows away.

October — Many summer flowers may continue to bloom but unless earlier flowers have been missed, the pressing season is over due to the dampness of the atmosphere at this time of year. This is the month to start collecting autumn leaves, especially from creepers. The smaller leaves of wild rose, dog weed, wayfarer, blackberry and hawthorn begin to change from green to shades of yellow, pink and maroon at this time of the year. They never fail to press beautifully and so it is at a time when flowers are scarce that I concentrate on leaf collecting from the hedgerow and garden. Grasses may also be found, dried by the sun to honey shades.

November	Mosses	green		These attractive shapes turn to pale green or honey colour.

Month	Plant	Colour		
December	Old Man's Beard seed heads	grey		Remove tiny seeds and press the fluff.

Flowers of potted houseplants or florists' flowers may be pressed:

	Begonia (small)	pink, red	*c*	Fade but interesting shape.
	Bougainvillea	pink, mauve	*c* *pw*	
	Cyclamen	pink, mauve, red	*c*	Press flower only.
	Impatiens	red, pink, white, bi-coloured	*c*	Pressed flower fades, but keeps colour at edge.
	Poinsettia	red, pink, white	*c*	Press bracts separately.
	Saintapaulia	purple	*c* *pw*	Press flower only.

A list of protected wild flowers is below and these species should not be picked or uprooted.

Species of protected plants

Common name	Scientific name
Alpine Gentian	Gentiana nivalis
Alpine Sow-thistle	Cicerbita alpina
Alpine Woodsia	Woodsia alpina
Blue Heath	Phyllodoce caerulea
Cheddar Pink	Dianthus gratianopolitanus
Diapensia	Diapensia lapponica
Drooping Saxifrage	Saxifraga cernua
Ghost Orchid	Epipogium aphyllum
Killarney Fern	Trichomanes speciosum
Lady's-slipper	Cypripedium calceolus
Mezereon	Daphne mezereum
Military Orchid	Orchis militaris
Monkey Orchid	Orchis simia
Oblong Woodsia	Woodsia ilvensis
Red Helleborine	Cephalanthera rubra
Snowdon Lily	Lloydia serotina
Spiked Speedwell	Veronica spicata
Spring Gentian	Gentiana verna
Teesdale Sandwort	Minuartia stricta
Tufted Saxifrage	Saxifraga cespitosa
Wild Gladiolus	Gladiolus illyricus

Notes